THE TIDEPOOL AND THE STARS

THE TIDEPOOL AND THE STARS

The Ecological Basis of Steinbeck's Depression Novels

Frederick Feied

Copyright © 2001 by Frederick Feied.

ISBN #:   Softcover   0-7388-6576-1

All rights reserved. No part of this book may be reproduced or transmitted in any form or by any means, electronic or mechanical, including photocopying, recording, or by any information storage and retrieval system, without permission in writing from the copyright owner.

This book was printed in the United States of America.

To order additional copies of this book, contact:
Xlibris Corporation
1-888-7-XLIBRIS
www.Xlibris.com
Orders@Xlibris.com

CONTENTS

INTRODUCTION 9

IN DUBIOUS BATTLE: DOC-THE
    NON-TELEOLOGICAL STANCE 17

IN DUBIOUS BATTLE: MAC AND JIM-
    The Teleological Committment 35

OF MICE AND MEN 53

THE GRAPES OF WRATH: The Thirties 66

THE GRAPES OF WRATH:
    Exodus and Migration 80

CONCLUSION 99

ENDNOTES 111

For Barbara, my Ed Ricketts.

INTRODUCTION

IN THE CONCLUDING CHAPTER OF *Exile's Return* Malcolm Cowley had the following comment to make on the 1930s: "The 1930s were the Pentecostal years when it seemed that everyone had the gift of tongues and used it to prophesy the millennium."(1) Among the host of writers who seemed to possess this gift, none appeared in the popular imagination to embody it more perfectly than John Steinbeck, whose novels on the marginal workers and dust bowl refugees appeared to take as their text the Biblical exhortation, "Awake and sing, ye that dwell in dust."

Between 1936 and 1939 Steinbeck published, in rapid succession, *In Dubious Battle*, *Of Mice and Men*, and *The Grapes of Wrath*—three novels dealing with the struggles and sufferings of the homeless and the dispossessed. The theme had never seemed more appropriate, for the 'thirties was a time of vast discontents when millions of hungry and homeless persons roved ceaselessly over the land, looking for a place to take root. It was a time when the spirits of men were borne low and a sense of defeat hung over everyone. Everywhere one saw soup kitchens and Hoovervilles, bonus marchers and apple sellers, and through it all, like a heavy underlining of tragedy, the long shabby ranks of the unemployed waiting before barred doorways. Drought and flood on an unprecedented scale had deepened and made sharper the general sense of misery occasioned by the collapse of the economic system. Men watched the headlines anxiously as though awaiting an amnesty or moved with the angry crowds which gathered to hear any speaker who thought he could offer an answer.

To a nation suffering general economic collapse Steinbeck's works seemed to come as a fitting literary echo to one of the most widely quoted expressions of the decade: "I see one-third of a nation ill-housed, ill-clad, ill-nourished." These words were uttered by Franklin Delano Roosevelt, "not in despair," as he told the nation, but "in hope," and in the Pentecostal spirit of the times it would have seemed contrary, not to say contentious, to suggest that Steinbeck was neither with nor of his times or that his vision, which could break forth in utterance of almost Hebraic grandeur, was of an ultimately different order.

But the mantle of prophet or disciple of social salvation rests uneasily on John Steinbeck's shoulders, for although each of these novels reveals an obvious concern with the plight of the exploited and underprivileged, the theme of social protest by no means exhausts their possibilities or comprehends the larger meanings implicit in the works.

Men gather sustenance where they may and take their moral support where they can find it. The 'thirties took from Steinbeck what the 'thirties needed, and men tended to see in his novels a scathing indictment of exploitation and a plea for social justice. That view, self-consistent as it may be on one level, fails to suggest the deeper significance of Steinbeck's thought. For despite the apparent primacy of the social frame of reference, Steinbeck's handling of his theme goes far beyond the limits of social interpretation. It is not traditional social philosophy, but biological science that dominates in his thought, and he sees his disinherited protagonists not as an economic by-product but as a biological excess.

Steinbeck's reputation rests largely on the three depression novels—*In Dubious Battle*, *Of Mice and Men*, and *The Grapes of Wrath* together with *Sea of Cortez*, a philosophical treatise and log of a biological expedition, which he wrote in collaboration with his friend Ed Ricketts, the marine biologist. These works have proved a continuing source of puzzlement to critics and laymen alike and have been subjected to a number of widely differing interpretations which vary according to the level of culture on which the judgment is made or the period in which it is issued. Each period has seen his work in a different light, and if early critics went to one extreme in interpreting his works as a call for a social uprising, later critics sometimes went to the opposite pole of depicting him as heartless and amoral.

Steinbeck's disappointment at the critical treatment he received is well known. In a letter to the editors of *The Colorado Quarterly* he once described criticism as "a kind of ill tempered parlor game in which nobody gets kissed."(2) Not long after, he wrote to another editor engaged in compiling a collection of Steinbeck criticism:

> "It is interesting to me that so many critics instead of making observations, are led to bring charges. It is not observed that I find it valid to understand man as an animal before I am prepared to know him as man. It is charged that I have somehow outraged members of my species by considering them part of a species at all. And how often the special pleaders use my work as a distorted echo chamber for their own ideas!"(3)

Steinbeck achieved international renown in his own lifetime, but he remains one of the most misunderstood writers in American literature. He enjoyed the dubious distinction of being called a Communist in the 'thirties, a Fascist in the 'forties, and a Social Darwinist in the 'sixties, all on the basis of the same body of work. The writer who could manage such violent swings all within the space of five years must be considered unique in the history of letters, but all such interpretations depend upon an analysis which examines separately elements which exist in dynamic opposition in Steinbeck's thought. In the absence of a theory capable of striking and maintaining a proper balance between these elements, his novels remained open to any interpretation however ill conceived or ill informed.

The problem that plagued earlier critics plagued the later ones as well. Briefly stated it was how to reconcile the social concern manifested in *The Grapes of Wrath* with the allegedly "Social Darwinist" doctrine which, as one critic put it, "dominates" both *In Dubious Battle* which preceded it in 1936 and *Sea of Cortez* which followed it in 1941.

Various attempts, all of them unsuccessful, were made to resolve this seeming contradiction. Some went so far as to draw a line down the middle of the depression novels, dividing them into different phases or periods. It was argued that *Sea of Cortez* clearly heralded a turning away from the social concerns of the 'thirties and a shift toward a detached and amoral philosophy based on "is" thinking. However, no satisfactory explanation could be given for the appearance of *In Dubious Battle* (which Steinbeck himself admitted had no "author's point of view") so early in the cycle.

But *Sea of Cortez* did not break with the past or initiate a new line of reasoning. Rather, it summed up and gave philosophical finish to ideas which had been the subject of considerable speculation between Ricketts and Steinbeck all during the 'thirties. In June of 1941 while he was still at work on the manuscript of *Sea of Cortez* Steinbeck made it clear that he regarded it as belonging to the works of this period, as a part of a cycle, as part of a whole. In a letter to his publisher Pascal Covici he wrote: "When this work is done I will have finished a cycle of work that has been biting me for many years."

It is impossible to account for the tone of Steinbeck's work in this period unless the influence of Ed Ricketts is taken into account. It was in 1930 that Steinbeck and Ricketts met—in a dentist's office as Steinbeck tells us in his short piece, "About Ed Ricketts." Instantly attracted to one another, they became close friends, and in time Steinbeck became a partner in Ricketts' marine laboratory in Monterey. By all accounts Ricketts was a remarkable individual. His intelligence, originality, and charm are attested to by all who came to know him. Almost twenty years after his death one could still find references to him and stories about him in the small newspapers of the Monterey peninsula. As Steinbeck put it, "he haunts the people who knew him."

One can only speculate as to the precise extent to which the concepts underlying Steinbeck's fiction originated with Ricketts, but "non-teleological philosophy", or "is" thinking—a non-judgmental approach to the study of human behavior—owes a great deal to his writing. There is considerable evidence to support his claim that "99 44/100%"

of the essay on non-teleological thinking in *Sea of Cortez* was his own and that the book contained numerous excerpts from his other unpublished works. But the two men worked so closely during this period that, as Steinbeck later recalled in the essay "About Ed Ricketts,"

> "Very many conclusions Ed and I worked out together through endless discussion and reading and observation and experiment. We worked together, and so closely that I do not now know in some cases who started which line of speculation since the end thought was the product of both minds. I do not know whose thought it was." (4)

The correspondence between the two men's ideas could hardly be greater. Fundamental to their system of ideas is the belief in the primacy of the biological sphere and the conviction that economic competition is only a special case under biological competition. The novels of this period view economic, political and social behavior from the vantage point of a non-teleological, non-judgmental philosophy which is firmly grounded in biological fundamentals as Darwin might have conceived them. The novels attempt to show the inter-relation and organic nature of the economic as well as the biological process.

In the course of any writer's career sudden breaks with the past in which all trace of transitional or residual influences are banished are probably the exception rather than the rule. Elements which either persist from the past or predict the future development are likely to be present at any given moment in a writer's work. This certainly holds true for Steinbeck. Certain themes which are present in the depression works are also to be found in either embryonic or degenerated form in works which precede or follow. Thus *Cup of Gold*, published in 1929, contains a fleeting allusion to group animals, and *To A God Unknown*, which appeared in 1933, deals with a character possessed of a kind of primitive sense of identity with the universe—both hallmarks of Steinbeck's work in the depression cycle

But what distinguishes *In Dubious Battle* from Steinbeck's earlier work and marks it as the starting point of a new phase in his career is its ecological emphasis, its non-teleological approach, its attempt to consider contemporary social relations in the light of our understanding of biological relationships. It is the systematic exploration and elaboration of these ideas that sets off *In Dubious Battle* and the works that follow from his early work. This consistent ecological overview, this non-teleological methodology and uncompromising biological emphasis marks the depression novels off from the later works as well. For although non-teleological heroes or themes persist in Steinbeck's work for some time after *Sea of Cortez*, such novels as *The Moon Is Down*, *Cannery Row*, and *The Wayward Bus* only pay lip service to the non-teleological philosophy. The approaching end of Steinbeck's interest in such themes is perhaps signalized by the increasingly routine and perfunctory treatment he gives them in these novels. They tend to be mere exercises in which the non-teleological element is only a thin veneer on a story which could be told equally well without it

In the letter to Pascal Covici cited above, Steinbeck went on to say that *The Sea of Cortez* was also "the careful statement of the thesis of work to be done in the future," but it seems clear that circumstances ruled otherwise. The outbreak of war brought a shift in mood and interests, and the death of Ed Ricketts in 1940 seemed to have effectively put an end to any such hopes or aspirations. Although he continued for a time to work the non-teleological vein, Steinbeck was never able to recapture the spirit or essence of the non-teleological method or to equal his earlier achievement.

The three depression novels reflect Steinbeck's biological and non-teleological commitment and the uncompromising philosophical naturalism he adopted as a conscious stance in that period. In that body of work he sought consistently and conscientiously to see and present the larger picture. Between 1934 when he commenced work on *In Dubious Battle* and 1941 when *The Sea of Cortez* appeared, he turned to illuminate first one and then the other side of the holistic equation, balancing theme against theme, treatment against treatment.

Thus, from the "brutal" objectivity of *In Dubious Battle*, which was published in March of 1936, he turned to the expose' of conditions among the migrant population of California, the hated "Okies," in a series which appeared in October of the same year in the *San Francisco News*, ("Their Blood is Strong" "Harvest Gypsies"). In *Of Mice and Men*, 1937, he once again examined the illusory nature of utopian or millennial aspirations—though the mood was noticeably softer than that of *In Dubious Battle*. Following this, in 1939, he published *The Grapes of Wrath*, in which he took pains to present the "author's moral point of view" which he had excluded from *In Dubious Battle*—only to return once more to the philosophically rigorous and scientifically detached treatment in *Sea of Cortez* (1941).

That this was a precarious balance which Steinbeck sought to maintain is clear on the face of it. In the fall of 1937, wrought to savage indignation at the plight of the starving migrants, he wrote to his agent, Elizabeth Otis:

> "I must go over into the interior valleys. There are five thousand families starving to death over there, not just hungry but actually starving. The government is trying to feed them and get medical attention for them, with the Fascist groups of utilities and banks and huge growers sabotaging the thing all along the line, and yelling for a balanced budget. In one tent there are twenty people quarantined for smallpox and two of the women are to have babies in that tent this week. I've tied into the thing from the first and I must get down there and see it and see if I can do something to knock these murderers on the heads."

But the evidence seems to suggest that he did his best to maintain his balance and to preserve, in the midst of turmoil, the objectivity necessary if he was to see the whole picture. Therein, perhaps, lies the full significance of his decision to destroy the early manuscript draft of *The Grapes of Wrath* which had been tentatively entitled *L'Affaire Lettuceberg*. Concerning this decision, a costly one for both publisher and writer, he wrote to his agent and publisher, "My whole work drive has been aimed at making people understand each other and then I deliberately write this book, the aim of which is to cause hatred through partial understanding."

In one sense Steinbeck is as contemporary as today, for the themes he so brilliantly explored in the works of this period seem destined to dominate in our lives for some time to come. Although recent ecological studies have taught us a great deal about the interdependence of all life forms on earth, Steinbeck and Ricketts may have made a unique contribution to our understanding of ourselves. As the forthcoming chapters will show, they offer insights into the nature of certain kinds of errors in human thought, errors which persist in the thinking of many if not most of our leading thinkers.

Anyone who examines the pronouncements of our statesmen, philosophers, even, on occasion, scientists will discover that with all too few exceptions such leaders are still bound by the iron strictures of a teleological habit of thought that has cost mankind dear in the past and threatens to drive it into extinction in the future.

IN DUBIOUS BATTLE: DOC—
THE NON-TELEOLOGICAL STANCE

In terms of mood and execution *In Dubious Battle* is clearly a product of the 'thirties. Structure and style are functional, stripped down to the essentials. Gone are the technical virtuosity and verbal pyrotechnics which distinguished the standard product of the 'twenties. Instead, Steinbeck employs what has been described as a kind of literary primitivism, as though to suggest that men in desperate times, driven as they were by hunger and haunted by fear, had a need to cleave deep to the tangible and the real and to speak in the unadorned language of the common man.

On one level *In Dubious Battle* reads like a typical depression novel. Two thousand crop tramps are camped in the Torgas Valley to pick the fruit crop when the Growers' Association announces a cut in pay. The Communist Party details two men—one a veteran organizer, the other a newly-joined apprentice—to work among the migrants and to help organize a strike. The strike is called and is broken in blood and violence which claims the life of Jim Nolan, the younger of the two Communists, as well as that of several other men. As the novel closes, Mac, the remaining Communist, seeks to exhort the men to put up a last-ditch fight against a threatened invasion of police and vigilantes.

In Dubious Battle is smoking hot with the passions of engagement. It is a study of class war and the Communist Party is in it up to the hilt. Despite the fact that it deals with events that are now remote it seems as contemporary as the morning newspaper. To read it is to be thrust with rude force into an epoch when danger was a commonplace, despair a constant. It summons up, as perhaps no other work of the period, the sense of menace as well as promise that hung in the air—the oppressive threat of fascism and the millennial exaltation of socialism: "There was a kind of ecstasy in him," (1) Mac says of his dead comrade, shot down by a sniper's bullet.

If this were all there were to the novel it would stand as a document of its times and Steinbeck, despite minor differences with the orthodox left, would stand forth as a novelist with a message, a novelist of social protest. But *In Dubious Battle* deals with what are apparently three levels of reality or perception at the same time—the biological or ecological, the sociological, and the ideological, and in order to comprehend what Steinbeck is about one must understand what he conceives to be the nature of the relationship between the three as well as the significance of the events he describes within each one.

To a remarkable degree, in both form and content, *In Dubious Battle* reflects the shape of Steinbeck's philosophical ideas in this period. A close examination of the structure as well as the argument of the novel makes clear that in Steinbeck's eyes the ideological and the economic (or sociological) spheres of influence or activity are subordinate to the biological. Economic conflict is an extension, outgrowth or expression of biological conflict and is subject to the same basic laws-laws which govern the behavior of all life forms. The difference is that man has developed certain highly sophisticated and arcane arithmetical formulations which disguise the process and put it at one remove.

Thus, the struggle between the strikers and the fruit growers, which appears at first glance to have the economic conflict as its primary or exclusive frame of reference, is seen to be only a special case under biological conflict. It takes place within the still larger and more significant context of the biological struggle for survival of which neither side is particularly aware.

In like manner, the war between the classes provides both setting and context for a clash of ideas between Mac, the Communist organizer, and Doc, his intellectual antagonist, physician to the striking crop tramps. The question which the two men consider, in one aspect or another, is the identical one of the primacy of existential levels—and their debate goes to the very heart of the philosophical ideas which Steinbeck, in collaboration with Ed Ricketts, was to develop at length in *The Sea of Cortez*.

In the confrontations between Doc and Mac, Steinbeck pairs the man of thought against the man of deeds—the observer who, as one of the minor characters says of himself, wants "to know things without believing them," (that is, without closing his mind) (IDB,16)—against the actor who both believes and acts on his beliefs. The opposition of the two men is consistent in the highest degree: observer versus actor, scientist versus organizer. As the one is concerned to discover what "is" the other is determined to achieve what "ought" to be. As the one speaks for the individual consciousness the other acts for what he conceives to be the group welfare.

Every aspect of their thought and behavior stands as an embodiment of the opposing systems of ideas of which they are representatives—the Darwinian and the social-utopian. In Steinbeck's eyes biological or Darwinian science gives rise to the kind of thinking which he describes as non-teleological, while utopian or millennial movements, whether secular or religious, he sees as ultimately teleological. Thus, on the philosophical or ideological level, Doc and Mac function as representatives or personifications of the two opposed ways of thinking—the non-teleological and the teleological.

In *Sea of Cortez*, Steinbeck tells us what he understands by the term non-teleological:

> "Non-teleological ideas derive through 'is' thinking associated with natural selection as Darwin seems to have understood it. They imply depth, fundamentalism, and clarity—seeing beyond traditional or personal projections. They consider events as outgrowths and expressions rather than as results; conscious acceptance as a desideratum, and certainly as an all-important prerequisite. Non-teleological thinking concerns itself

primarily not with what should be, or could be, or might be, but rather with what actually 'is'—attempting at most to answer the already sufficiently difficult questions *what* or *how*, instead of *why*." (2)

Doc Burton illustrates this attitude in the first serious conversation he holds with Mac. When Mac asks him if he does not "think the cause is good?" Doc responds by saying: "I don't want to put on the blinders of 'good' and 'bad' and limit my vision." (IDB, 149) When Mac, speaking in sociological terms, asks Doc heatedly, "How about social injustice? The profit system? You have to say they're bad," Doc's answer comes in biological terms "Look at the physiological injustice," he tells Mac, "the injustice of tetanus, the injustice of syphilis, the gangster methods of amoebic dysentery—that's my field." (IDB,150) And when Mac tells him that it is different because "men are doing one, and germs are doing the other," Doc answers, "I can't see much difference, Mac." (IDB, 150)

Doc does not mean to suggest that we ought to regard the behavior of the tetanus bacteria as unfair or that we ought to describe the amoeba which causes dysentery as behaving in a lawless way, but that just as we recognize the irrelevance of such terms when we are trying to understand the behavior of bacteria we ought to recognize their ultimate irrelevance when the subject is the study of man. He clearly implies that their use in a human context is no more valid than their use in a bacterial context and in so doing he is illustrating a fundamental tenet of non-teleological thinking.

The larger point is, of course, that in both cases we are dealing with organisms which have survived by virtue of their ability to compete successfully in the environment in which they exist. They exist, in fact, only because of that ability. It is therefore unreasonable and irrational to ascribe evil motives to men *or* microbes because of the way they interact with their environment in their efforts to survive. What point could there be in pronouncing such judgments on man or microbe when the nature of every living creature has, in a profound sense, been shaped by that very interaction and has evolved over the eons in obedience to natural laws which go far deeper than man-made laws or customs.

In *Sea of Cortez* Steinbeck goes even further to suggest not only the pointlessness but the absurdity of value judgments, to human as well as to animal behavior. Everywhere he looks in nature he sees a vital competition in which creatures contend with one another for survival. This is natural, this is basic, he tells us: "The forms and species and units and groups are armed for survival, fanged for survival, timid for it, fierce for it, clever for it, poisonous for it, intelligent for it." (SC, 96)

But man has created a situation in which he is unable to look at himself realistically, and "in our structure of society" the qualities which "are invariable concomitants of failure" are "considered good qualities" while those which "are the cornerstones of success" are regarded as "the bad ones."

"In an animal other than man," Steinbeck suggests, "we would replace the term 'good' with 'weak survival quotient.'" (SC, 241)

In his view, "Life has one final end, to be alive; and all the tricks and mechanisms, all the successes and all the failures, are aimed at that end." (SC,241) Thus, what Mac regards as "injustice,"—the aggressions of class against class, group against group—Steinbeck, or Doc, regards as the inevitable process of life, the expected, the given. Such conflicts have no intrinsic or absolute value inherent in them. They are to be studied dispassionately, to be reported objectively. They are as soulless, as directionless, as purposeless as the conflicts between two specimens of marine life in a tide pool. To put it in terms of Doc's discussion with Mac—it makes no difference that men are doing one and germs are doing the other. The struggle for survival takes place on all levels, and though it may take different forms on different levels of life, it is nevertheless common to them all.

In Doc's view, all life is a Darwinian battleground. It is clear that infection represents a direct struggle or competition for survival on the biological level. It seems equally clear to Doc that the competition for survival on the sociological level is a corollary of competition on the biological. In his eyes the economic struggle, although conducted within the framework of man's social institutions, remains at bottom a biological competition, for the very organizations men form to help them in the battle against nature also find it necessary to compete against one another. In a sense men prey on one another just as the lower orders do in order to secure a share of the necessities of life for themselves and their offspring. If there is drought or flood or depression, the competition and the resulting conflict will be intensified. But in any event, since the fruitfulness of nature tends to assure the fact that the offspring of any given species, unless held in check, will increase faster than the available food supply, the conflict tends to be fierce and unremitting.

The point which Doc makes on the philosophical level, Steinbeck supports on the phenomenal level. Even before the conversation between Doc and Mac is allowed to begin Steinbeck illustrates the point subliminally, so to speak:

"A barn owl, screeching overhead with a ripping sound startled the men.

'That's an owl, Jim,' Mac explained. 'He's hunting mice.'

And then to Burton. 'Jim's never been in the country much. The things we know are new to him.'" (IDB, 148)

Again, when the body of Mac's murdered comrade, Joy, is first brought back to the hobo camp we are treated to the illuminating spectacle of man killing and being killed, eating and being eaten.

"London stood up heavily. His wide blue shirt-front was streaked with Joy's blood. Burton took one look at Joy. 'Killed 'im, eh?'

'Got him,' said London.

Burton said, 'Bring him to my tent. I'll look him over.' From behind the tents a hoarse, bubbling scream broke out. All of the men turned, frozen at the sound. Burton said, 'Oh, they're killing a pig. One of the cars brought back a live pig. Bring this body to my tent.'" (IDB, 174)

All though the following scene while the strikers decide what to do with Joy's body, whether to send him to the morgue or to refuse to turn him over to the authorities, references to the slaughtered pig are slyly introduced.

"Dakin lifted the flap and stepped into the big tent. 'They're fryin' pork,' he said. 'They sure cut up that pig quick.' Mac said, 'Dakin, can you have the guys build a kind of platform? We'll want some place for the coffin to set.'" (IDB, 174-75)

Shortly thereafter the county coroner arrives demanding his corpse. As Mac and Jim walk toward the stoves where the pork is being cooked, two men pass carrying the body of Joy between them, and the coroner walked fussily along behind.

"Men were walking away from the stoves with pieces of greasy fried pork in their hands. They wiped their lips with their sleeves. The tops of the stoves were covered with little slabs of hissing meat. 'God that smells good,' said Mac. 'Let's get some. I'm hungry as hell.' The cooks handed out ill-cut, half-cooked pieces of pork to them, and they strolled away, gnawing at the soft meat." (IDB, 179)

"Your worm is your only emperor for diet," Hamlet observes: "We fat all else to fat us, and we fat ourselves for maggots." At Joy's burial Steinbeck indulges his opportunity to make this point. As Joy is about to be fed to the worms, the strikers learn that two cows and one bull calf have been donated to their kitchen. At the cemetery Mac receives a note instructing him to send some men to butcher the animals.

"'Two cows and a calf. Ten sacks of beans! Why the guys can go right out in this truck now.' From the crowded side of the cemetery came the beating of mud thrown down on the pine casket.

'Y'see,' Mac said. 'The guys'll feel fine when they get their stomachs full of meat and beans.'

London said, 'I could do with a piece of meat myself,'" (IDB, 237)

"Everything," Steinbeck comments in *Sea of Cortez*, "ate everything else with a furious exuberance." (SC, 47) Steinbeck does not see this process or struggle as evil or unjust; he sees it as an enduring and necessary condition of life. In his view, "all life is based on such a postulate." (SC, 134)

Steinbeck was apparently somewhat sensitive to the charge that non-teleological thinking is cruel and inhuman. "This type of thinking unfortunately annoys many people," he remarked in *Sea of Cortez*. "It may especially arouse the anger of women, who regard it as cold, even brutal." (SC, 133) In another place he speaks of the fact that "whoever employs this type of thinking with other than a few close friends will be referred to as detached, hard-hearted, or even cruel." (SC, 146) However, to him "quite the opposite seems to be true. Non-teleological methods more than any other seem capable of great tenderness, of an all-embracingness which is rare otherwise." (SC, 146)

Thus, Doc's behavior, while appearing at first glance to be cold or unfeeling, gives flesh to Steinbeck's thesis that non-teleological thinking is "more tender and understanding, certainly more real and less illusionary and even less blaming, than the conventional methods of consideration." (SC, 133) Doc is involved in no violence. As physician to the striking crop tramps he moves among them practicing the healing arts. He refuses to put on the blinders of "good" and "bad." He refuses to lay blame.

The significance of Doc's refusal to lay blame becomes clear when it is seen that in the conflict between the crop tramps and the fruit growers both groups throw the blame on the other side and justify the slaughter which is about to take place on the grounds that they are defending their children. Just before the threatened attack by the vigilantes, the president of the Fruit Growers' Association tells London, the strike leader:

> "Can't you see that if you attack our homes and our children we have to protect them? Wouldn't you protect your own children?"
> "What the hell do you think we're doin'" London cried. "We're trying to protect 'em from starving. We're using the only way a workin' stiff's got." (IDB, 253)

The contrast with Doc's thinking and behavior is clear. In the name of justice the two parties, locked in a struggle for survival, pronounce sentence on each other and proceed to carry out a policy of mutual extermination. An economic difference turns into a biological conflict to destroy or eliminate the opposition. While claiming to be concerned with "good" and "justice" both groups, in fact, carry out policies which lead to widespread pain and suffering.

Steinbeck goes to some lengths to clear Doc of any implication of cold-bloodedness or lack of sympathy. In fact, he is at some pains to show him as essentially tender and warmhearted in all his personal relations. But it is important to understand that Doc's refusal to lay blame in the fruit picker's strike is not a case of simple tolerance reflecting a kindly and congenial disposition, but that it derives instead from a rigorous and all-pervasive philosophical position which denies the possibility of laying blame because it denies the very concept of causality itself.

It is Steinbeck's contention that causality is "merely a name for something that exists only in our partial and biased mental reconstructings." (SC,149) He sees reality as relational rather than causational:

> "Usually it seems to be true that when even the most definitely apparent cause-effect situations are examined in the light of wider knowledge, the cause-effect aspect comes to be seen as less rather than more significant, and the statistical or relational aspects acquire larger importance." (SC, 141)

He argues that only the totality is valid. "The separate reasons," he tells us, "no matter how valid, are only fragmentary parts of the picture." (SC, 149)

In the following example he asks us to "note the deep significance of the emergent as contrasted with the presumably satisfactory but actually incorrect original naive understanding," which produced the opposite effect from that which was intended.

> "At one time an important game bird in Norway, the willow grouse, was so clearly threatened with extinction

that it was thought wise to establish protective regulations and to place a bounty on its chief enemy, a hawk which was known to feed heavily on it. Quantities of the hawks were exterminated, but despite such drastic measures the grouse disappeared actually more rapidly than before. The naively applied customary remedies had obviously failed. But instead of becoming discouraged and quietistically letting this bird go the way of the great auk and the passenger pigeon, the authorities enlarged the scope of their investigations until the anomaly was explained. An ecological analysis into the relational aspects of the situation disclosed that a parasitic disease, coccidiosis, was endemic among the grouse. In its incipient stages, this disease so reduced the flying speed of the grouse that the mildly ill individuals became easy prey for the hawks. In living largely off the slightly ill birds, the hawks prevented them from developing the disease in its full intensity and so spreading it more widely and quickly to otherwise healthy fowl. Thus the presumed enemies of the grouse, by controlling the epidemic aspects of the disease, proved to be friends in disguise." (SC, 144-45)

By examples such as these Steinbeck would direct our attention to the presence of factors, "separately not important or not yet discovered, which in the aggregate may be significant, or the integration of which may be found to wash over some critical threshold." (SC, 136)

To the extent that one understands this, one tends less and less to be satisfied with partial "answers" and to seek instead to comprehend the larger and larger picture. For "in the non-teleological sense"—that is, in a proper study of what "is" unhampered by *a priori* reasoning concerning design, plan or forethought in the universe, Steinbeck tells us, "there can be no 'answer.' There can only be pictures which become larger and more significant as one's horizon increases." (SC, 136)

Thus, in Steinbeck's view, the impulse to lay blame can only arise out of an incomplete comprehension which leads one to infer a causality, and therefore a responsibility, which is in fact not present. The circularity of the argument is complete. Causality, based on incomplete or partial understanding leads to value judgments or blame. Or to reverse the direction of the argument: value judgments represent a kind of praise or blame deriving from a sense of responsibility or causality based on an incomplete comprehension of the whole.

This vicious circularity Steinbeck sees as both the condition for and the concomitant of all teleologies. He would oppose to this a kind of dialectical process in which thesis and antithesis yield to synthesis. In this process. the non-teleological picture

> ". . . is the larger one that goes beyond blame or cause. And the non-causal or non-blaming viewpoint seems to us very often relatively to represent the 'new thing,' . . .which arises emergently from the union of two opposing viewpoints. . . especially if there is a conflict as to causation between the two or within either. The new viewpoint very frequently sheds light over a larger picture, providing a key which may unlock levels not accessible to either of the teleological viewpoints." (SC, 148)

But in the shortsighted view which customarily prevails among homogenous value groups, each side believes that it understands the causes of the conflicts. Each sees the other's intransigence as the cause of the difficulty: each is therefore convinced of the other's guilt. Thus, in the conflict between the fruit tramps and the fruit growers both groups have accepted a partial answer. Both groups have available a more or less highly perfected social analysis by which to explain the cause of the conflict and pin the guilt on the other side; both have at least the rudiments of an ideology. In the course of the strike they elaborate a group code and enforce a group discipline.

So all pervasive is this group influence that as Doc observes the evolution of the strike he puts forward the notion that the strikers have assumed roles in a new entity which is different from a simple collection of individual men and which he calls "group-man." He tells Mac: "A man in a group isn't himself at all; he's a cell in an organism that isn't like him any more than the cells in your body are like you." (IDB, 150-51)

Doc wants to study this new entity, group-man, for it appears to him "to be a new individual, not at all like single men." (IDB, 150) He tells Mac, "it might be worthwhile to know more about group-man, to know his nature, his ends, his desires. They're not the same as ours," (IDB, 152)

Mac is unable to see the relevance of Doc's comments about group-man to the practical problems at hand. "What's all this kind of talk got to do with hungry men, with lay-offs and unemployment?'" he demands at one point. Doc's answer to Mac might well have been taken to heart by Steinbeck's critics who have, by and large, tended to dismiss Steinbeck's ideas with the same impatient contempt Mac accords to Doc's. He tells Mac: "It might have a great deal to do with them. It isn't a very long time since tetanus and lockjaw were not connected. There are still primitives in the world who don't know children are the result of intercourse." (IDB, 152)

The concept of group-man was perhaps the most provocative and controversial notion Steinbeck elaborated in the novel, and one which was to lay him open to charges which included everything from scientism to mysticism. But it seems clear that what Steinbeck means to suggest is that certain patterns of behavior are imposed on the group by the iron requirements of survival. Those which fail to meet those requirements simply fail of survival, and since, particularly among the higher orders, the exigencies of survival make imperative a system whereby the group may, in the face of danger, act as a single unit, controlling the behavior of the individual members or causing those members to act in a certain way, those groups most successfully meeting this challenge would be most likely to survive. In the case of humans this need hastens on the creation of a body of customs, norms, value systems or ideologies which seek to inculcate the kind of behavior considered desirable from the point of view of group survival. Doc tells Mac:

> "When group-man wants to move, he makes a standard. 'God wills that we re-capture the Holy Land'; or he says, 'We fight to make the world safe for democracy'; or he says, 'we will wipe out social injustice with communism.' But the group doesn't care about the Holy Land, or Democracy, or Communism. Maybe the group simply wants to move, to fight, and uses these words simply to reassure the brains of individual men." (IDB, 151)

In *Sea of Cortez* Steinbeck returned to a consideration of certain aspects of group behavior as they pertain to marine biology. His findings and speculations reinforce the thesis put forward in *In Dubious Battle* and shed considerable light on the discussion between Doc and Mac.

During the course of his expedition to the Gulf of California, which he refers to by its earlier name, the Sea of Cortez, Steinbeck had occasion many times to observe the precision maneuvers of groups or schools of fish. At one point he writes:

> "We had never been in waters so heavily populated. The light, piercing the surface, showed the water almost solid with fish. . . . The school swam, marshaled and patrolled. They turned as a unit and dived as a unit. In their millions they followed a pattern minute as to direction and depth and speed." (SC, 240)

But such precision, Steinbeck notes, must seem incomprehensible to the observer who regards a school as simply millions of fish. He writes in words reminiscent of Doc Burton's:

> "There must be some fallacy in our thinking of these fish as individuals. Their functions in the school are in some as yet unknown way as controlled as though the school

were one unit. We cannot conceive of this intricacy until we are able to think of the school as an animal itself." (SC, 240)

In words that are almost a verbatim transcription of Doc's, Steinbeck and Ricketts suggest that "this larger animal, the school, seems to have a nature and drives and ends of its own. It reacts with all its cells to stimuli which perhaps might not influence one fish at all." (SC, 240)

The existence of such intricate and perhaps instinctive patterns of group behavior is again to be explained through the principle of natural selection. The penalty for failure of any group to conform to the required pattern being extinction, those behavioral patterns most conducive to survival are those most likely to be perpetuated. Such a pattern may in times become a highly refined response on the part of the creatures employing it, perhaps even calling forth a special adaptation as they evolve over countless eons in successful interaction with their environment.

Steinbeck writes about the school that:

> "It is more than and different from the sum of its units. If we can think this way, it will not seem so unbelievable that every fish heads in the same direction, that the water interval between fish and fish is identical with all units, and that it seems to be directed by a school intelligence. If it is a unit animal itself, why should it not so react? (SC, 240)

In his discussion with Mac, Doc suggests that if people could only learn to "look at mobs not as men, but as mobs," they would discover that "a mob nearly always seems to act reasonably, for a mob." (IDB, 151)

Once again Steinbeck seems to be saying that in the case of humans the norms of the group, operating on a homogenous collection of individuals, would tend to produce a kind of collective behavior since the tendency or proclivity to conform to whatever norm of group behavior is the current vogue is highly marked in men. The desire to conform and the techniques whereby to conform even to norms which fluctuate rapidly are developed early in childhood. Such skills are at first, perhaps, painfully and haltingly learned. But once learned they become more and more highly refined. Through the mechanism of the conditioned reflex, the proclivity or tendency to ascertain and conform to correct or prescribed group behavior in whatever situation may amount almost to a loss of personal identity, for it may become, in time, ingrained habit conditioned by constant sensory and intellectual bombardment to the point where it becomes part of an automatic stimulus-response pattern such as those described in Pavlov's celebrated experiments.

The behavior of schools of fish led Steinbeck to go further in speculating that there was even a division of roles, a specialization of functions to be observed within a school: "Perhaps this is the wildest of speculations, but we suspect that when the school is studied as an animal rather than as a sum of unit fish, it will be found that certain units are assigned special functions to perform." (SC, 240)

No one who has read Melville's account of the behavior of whales or who has had occasion to examine studies of the behavior of other mammals has any cause to doubt that certain individuals are assigned specific roles within the group and that females and the young, for example, are often encircled by a protective cordon of males when there is a threat of danger.(1)

In a book on marine biology also entitled *Sea of Cortez*, Ray Cannon offers an example of such specialization carried out to an amazing degree. In his account of the golden grouper he describes the way in which certain fish, clearly distinguished by their vivid coloring, perform the highly specialized function of rounding up and herding together the food supply for the entire group. Each fish in the school plays its part and maintains its position in an apparently well-rehearsed routine until the prey has been stunned and smashed by repeated assaults, at which time all members of the school dash in for the kill. (Menlo Park, Calif.: Lane Magazine & Book Co., 1966) p.203.

In Dubious Battle had earlier made a similar point. Mac attempts to confound Doc's thesis about group man by pointing to persons such as himself who played individual roles. He tells Doc, "You go too far with collectivization. How do you account for people like me, directing things, moving things? That puts your group-man out." (IDB, 151)

Doc counters with the argument concerning specialization of function:

> "You might be an effect as well as a cause, Mac. You might be an expression of group-man, a cell endowed with a special function, like an eye cell, drawing your force from group-man, and at the same time directing him, like an eye. Your eye both takes orders from and gives orders to your brain." (IDB, 151)

By thus equating specialization of social function with specialization of biological function Steinbeck perhaps attempts to suggest the essentially organic and interrelated nature of the social process as in *Sea of Cortez* he suggests the organic and interrelated nature of the biological or ecological process. There he describes a group of fish which, like the strikers of *In Dubious Battle*, appear to behave as unit animals, and in which certain individuals perform specialized functions for the whole. But the process does not stop there, for Steinbeck suggests that these groups exist in dynamic interrelation with even larger groups which in turn may play a part in the economy of the whole. Describing his experiences in the Bay of San Carlos, Steinbeck writes:

> "In the little Bay of San Carlos, where there were many schools of a number of species, there was even a feeling (and 'feeling' is used advisedly) of a larger unit which was the inter-relation of species with their interdependence for food, even though that food be each other. A smoothly working larger animal surviving within

itself—larval shrimp to little fish to giant fish—one operating mechanism. .And perhaps *this* unit of survival may key into the larger animal which is the life of all the sea, and this into the larger of the world." (SC, 241)

The implication seems to be plain. Once seen in its relational aspects, once comprehended in its totality, what point could there be to laying blame? The life process of each is dependant upon, is related to, the maintenance of ecological balance and harmony in the larger unit in which each is the food supply of the other, in which each in turn devours and is devoured by its neighbors.

Doc's refusal to lay blame in the fruit pickers' strike may be seen to grow out of his desire to see the whole in all its aspects, for, unpleasant as the notion may be to some, the social process, viewed in its totality, may likewise be seen as a balanced and interlocking whole in which everything plays its part, and in which no phenomenon, however isolated or insignificant, may be left out of account. Such a view faces up to the "facts as they are" and meets the requirements of non-teleological thinking which Steinbeck sees as calling for "conscious acceptance as a desideratum, and certainly as an all-important prerequisite." And in place of "a fierce but ineffectual attempt to change conditions which are assumed to be undesirable," Steinbeck calls for "the understanding-acceptance which would pave the way for a more sensible attempt at any change which might still be indicated." (SC, 135)

Steinbeck's depression novels are still being studied as examples of social protest. It seems clear, however, that Steinbeck does not stop at the investigation of human social organization, nor is it his ultimate concern to pass judgment on the equity of social institutions. But if the Steinbeck of this period was not a believer in utopias, neither was he a social Darwinist, a defender of the *status quo*, as the *San Francisco News* series, "The Harvest Gypsies," which began appearing in October 1936 eight months *after* the publication of *In Dubious Battle*, makes clear. In this series, later collected and published under the title, "Their

Blood Is Strong," Steinbeck calls for a far-reaching program to improve the lot and restore the rights of the migrant workers.

Steinbeck's behavior finds its parallel in that of his protagonist, for although neither believes in the millennium both feel a genuine concern for the plight of the migrants and put their skill at their disposal. Mac understood Doc far better than Steinbeck's contemporaries understood him. He pays him the highest tribute of which he is capable:

> "It's a funny thing, Doc. You don't believe in the cause, and you'll probably be the last man to stick. I don't get you at all."

Doc's answer may, perhaps, be taken as Steinbeck's own: "I don't believe in the cause, but I believe in men." (IDB, 200)

IN DUBIOUS BATTLE: MAC AND JIM-*THE TELEOLOGICAL COMMITTMENT*

Over against Doc Burton, observer and speculative thinker, spokesman for non-teleological thinking, Steinbeck places Mac, the political activist, organizer and leader of men, exemplar of a very different way of looking at things. Mac's thought and behavior accord perfectly with the definition of teleological thinking Steinbeck gives in *Sea of Cortez*:

> "What we personally conceive by the term teleological thinking,. . .is most frequently associated with the evaluating of causes and effects, the purposiveness of events. This kind of thinking considers changes and cures—what 'should be' in the terms of an end pattern(which is often a subjective or an anthropomorphic projection); it presumes the bettering of conditions, often, unfortunately, without achieving more than a most superficial understanding of those conditions. In their sometimes intolerant refusal to face facts as they are, teleological notions may substitute a fierce but ineffectual attempt to change conditions which are assumed to be undesirable, in place of the understanding-acceptance which would pave the way for a more sensible attempt at any change which might still be indicated."
> (SC, 134-35)

For Mac, the over-riding reality is the social reality. Whereas Doc refuses to place blame or assign responsibility and rejects the very notion of causality, Mac shows no reluctance to make value judgments, and he interprets the conflict around them as a conflict between the forces of good and evil. Mac believes in "the cause," in historical destiny and the inevitability of progress. Mac sees history as going somewhere, as building to something. History, in his view, is working to a final term product, to an end result, to a perfect, classless society. Mac's theory of history, therefore, gives him cause to hope for the coming of the millennium.

Steinbeck rejects such a view of history as "a subjective or an anthropomorphic projection"—an example of "causal thinking warped by hope." (SC, 86) Such "projections" or teleologies are not exclusively the property of the conventionally religious however. For "even those who have managed to drop the leading-strings of a Sunday-school deity are still led by the unconscious teleology of their developed trick." (SC,86)

Hope is "a diagnostic human trait," Steinbeck suggests and in thus hoping for the unattainable, Mac is only exhibiting or succumbing to a generic human failing. "This simple cortex symptom," Steinbeck remarks in *Sea of Cortez*,

> "seems to be a prime factor in our inspection of our universe. For hope implies a change from a present bad condition to a future better one. A slave hopes for freedom, the weary man hopes for rest, the hungry for food. And the feeders of hope, economic and religious, have managed to create a world picture which is very hard to escape." (SC, 86)

The particular form which such teleologies take may vary from one period to another or shift their emphasis according to whether they are founded in secular or religious beliefs. All of them, however, reveal a central core of belief or conviction in the purposiveness of the universe, of history or of social evolution.

> "Man grows toward perfection; animals grow toward man; bad grows toward good; and down toward up, until our little mechanism, hope, . . . manages to warp the whole world." (SC, 86)

Hope, which leads some to believe in salvation and to have faith in the possibility of attaining to a heavenly afterlife, leads Mac to believe in the millennium and to have faith in the possibility of attaining to an earthly paradise. The faith which others place in a deity, Mac reserves for history. Or, to put it another way, Mac finds God in history. It is this tendency to induce belief or faith that Steinbeck finds most objectionable in teleological thinking, for while such faith, even in the amount of the proverbial mustard seed, may feed the hope of life everlasting, it is a dose likely to prove fatal to intellectual inquiry.

> "But the greatest fallacy in, or rather the greatest objection to, teleological thinking is in connection with the emotional content, the belief. People get to believing and even to professing the apparent answers thus arrived at, suffering mental constrictions by emotionally closing their minds to any of the further and possibly opposite 'answers' which might otherwise be unearthed by honest effort—answers which, if faced realistically, would give rise to a struggle and to a possible rebirth which might place the whole problem in a new and more significant light." (SC, 143)

Doc rejects belief and refuses to put the blinders of "good" and "bad" precisely because he does not want to close his mind.

"Listen to me. Mac. My senses aren't above reproach, but they're all I have. I want to see the whole picture—as nearly as I can. I don't want to put on the blinders of 'good' and 'bad,' and limit my vision. If I used the term 'good' on a thing I'd lose my license to inspect it, because there might be bad in it. Don't you see? I want to be able to look at the whole thing." (IDB, 149)

Mac and Jim, on the other hand, are incapable of seeing "the whole thing" because their belief gets in the way. Failing to see "the whole picture" they inevitably end up in confusion. In a passage reminiscent of Henry Adams' treatment of Grant, Mazzini, and other political leaders, Doc tells Mac

> "You practical men always lead practical men with stomachs. And something always gets out of hand. Your men get out of hand, they don't follow the rules of common sense, and you practical men either deny that it is so, or refuse to think about it. And when someone wonders what it is that makes a man with a stomach something more than your rule allows, why you howl, 'Dreamer, mystic, metaphysician.' I don't know why I talk about it to a practical man. In all history there are no men who have come to such wild-eyed confusion and bewilderment as practical men leading men with stomachs." (IDB, 153)

Mac responds to Doc's diatribe with the time-honored contempt of the practical man: "We've got a job to do," Mac tells him. "We've got no time to mess around with high-falutin' ideas."

"Yes," Doc responds, "and so you start your work not knowing your medium. And your ignorance trips you up every time." (IDB, 153)

Steinbeck and Ricketts make Doc's point even more explicitly in *Sea Of Cortez*. The trouble with so-called "practical men" is that they have a tendency to commit themselves to policies and programs aimed at "bettering conditions" of which they have no more than "a most superficial understanding." (SC, 134-35} Practical men like Mac have accepted a partial answer and closed their minds to the larger picture. The belief or faith engendered by their hope impels them to construct their iron teleologies.

The "feeders of hope," as Steinbeck calls them, have much in common. Both "economic and religious" leaders or feeders of hope provide a sense of purpose, both provide a final goal, and both offer the possibility of rebirth.

Nowhere is this better illustrated than in the story of Jim Nolan. Jim is a tragic victim of the strike, but we are not instructed to feel sorry for him; we are not to understand that his life is a waste. Like many a martyr Jim finds in death his highest fulfillment

When we first meet Jim he is about to join the Communist Party because, as he tells his interviewer, "I felt dead. I thought I might get alive again." (IDB, 16) He describes how in a jail cell once he met several Communists whose lives he could not help contrasting with his own: "Everything's been a mess, all my life. Their lives weren't messes. They were working toward something. I want to work toward something." (IDB, 16)

Jim tells Mac of the larger vision which brought him to join the Party.

> "In that cell were five men all raised in about the same condition. Some of them worse, even. And while there was anger in them, it wasn't the same kind of anger. They didn't hate a boss or a butcher. They hated the whole system of bosses, but that was a different thing. It wasn't the same kind of anger. And there was something else, Mac. The hopelessness wasn't in them. They were quiet, and they were working; but in the back of every mind there was conviction that sooner or later they would win their way out of the system they hated. I tell you, there was a kind of peacefulness about those men." (IDB, 30-31)

In a sense Jim Nolan is reborn into a secular religion, but the young apostle of Communism denies all belief in religion or religious feeling. Nowhere does Steinbeck employ the subtle counterpoint of dialogue to better advantage than in the discussion between Doc and Jim on this point. We are treated to an instructive exercise in semantics. The words mean one thing to Doc—they mean quite another to Jim Nolan:

When Doc says "... you've got something in your eyes, Jim, something religious. I've seen it in you boys before." Jim flares up telling him, "Well, it isn't religious. I've got no use for religion." Doc responds: "Don't let me confuse you with terms. You're living the good life, whatever you want to call it."

When Jim confides in Doc that he is, "happy for the first time." Doc answers, "I know. Don't let it die. It's the vision of Heaven." Jim responds "I don't believe in Heaven ... I don't believe in religion." (IDB, 206)

The parallels between the two varieties of teleology extend even to the exhortatory or agitational techniques by which the faithful are roused to action. There is something unmistakably religious in the scene at Joy's funeral. Mac's words have an almost hypnotic effect on the strikers. As he addresses them he falls naturally into the pattern of incantation and response common to traditional religions. He tells them how many times Joy was beaten by the police—how his face was beaten to rags—how "his hands were broke, an' his jaw was broke." (IDB, 231) He tells them how once Joy lay in jail with a broken jaw because a doctor wouldn't treat "a Goddamn red."

"Suddenly he shouted, 'What are you going to do about it? Dump him in a mud-hole, cover him with slush. Forget him.'

A woman in the crowd began to sob hysterically.

'He was fightin' for you,' Mac shouted. 'You goin' to forget it?'

A man in the crowd yelled, 'No, by Christ!'

Mac hammered on, 'Goin' to let him get killed, while you lie down and take it?'

A chorus this time, 'No-o-o!'

Mac's voice dropped into a sing-song. 'Goin' to dump him in the mud?'

'No-oo.' The bodies swayed a little bit.

'He fought for you. Are you going to forget him?'

'No-o-o.'

'We're going to march through town. You going to let any damn cops stop us?'

The heavy roar, 'No-oo.' The crowd swayed in the rhythm. They poised for the next response." (IDB, 232)

Like Jim Nolan, Mac is annoyed when Doc Burton brings up the parallel to pulpit oratory.

"'You surely know how to work them, Mac,' he said quietly, 'No preacher ever brought people to the mourners' bench quicker. Why didn't you keep it up awhile? You'd've had them talking in tongues and holy-rolling in a minute.' Mac said irritably, 'Quit sniping at me, Doc. I've got a job to do and I've got to use every means to do it.'" (IDB, 233)

There is a sense in which Mac *is* using the means of traditional religious forms to achieve his own ends—the ends of revolutionary communism. But there is also a sense in which he himself is being used in an ever repeated pattern of the race.

Paradoxically, it is his vision of the millennium, his dream of social justice that steels Mac to his tasks even when they fill him with horror. Armed with his vision, Mac scruples at nothing. On one occasion, when the strikers bring in a young boy who had been caught on the point of firing a rifle into the camp, Mac makes an example of him:

> "His right fist worked in quick short hammer blows, one after another. The nose cracked flat, the other eye closed, and the dark bruises formed on the cheeks." (IDB, 273)

It would be a mistake to conclude from this that Steinbeck intends to portray Mac as a sadist. Far from it. Over and over again Mac tells us that he is just doing what he has to do. His cruelty is not the result of callousness but stems from his teleological commitment, and his behavior is intended to illustrate the brutality that is the inevitable accompaniment of teleological commitment. When the episode is over, Mac reacts with a spasm of uncontrollable horror:

"He walked to the mattress and sat down and clutched his knees. All over his body the muscles shuddered. His face was pale and grey." (IDB, 279)

Steinbeck's depiction of Mac's pragmatism, his cold-blooded realism, his tactical opportunism has sometimes been interpreted as an attack on the Communists. Critics left and right took sides on the issue-the left protesting the slander, the right smugly affirming its correctness. Neither side was prepared to recognize that what Steinbeck had done was to underscore a basic truth, as he saw it, about all teleologies, whether secular or religious.

Steinbeck and Ricketts recognized that, for better or for worse, teleologies are a part of the reality that one must deal with, and since, "Non-teleological thinking concerns itself not with what should be, or could be, or might be, but rather with what actually 'is'" (SC, 135) it cannot ignore the fact that as things stand, practical men play a major role in the affairs of the world. They cannot be left out of the account. If statesmen and practical men universally employ the 'limited and inadequate' teleological method of thinking, their method of approaching problems is still a factor to be taken account of in any assessment of the whole.

They acknowledge that, "Teleological 'answers' necessarily must be included in non-teleological method—since they are part of the picture even if only restrictedly true—and as soon as their qualities of relatedness are recognized. Even erroneous beliefs are real things, and have to be considered proportional to their spread and intensity."(SC, 144)

In Dubious Battle is consistent with the ideas put forward in *Sea of Cortez*. Regardless of whether Mac is mistaken or not, his beliefs are a force to be reckoned with. To the extent that he acts on them they will materially affect events and must be taken into account in the larger picture.

In the larger picture, in the all-embracing view of the totality aspired to by a non-teleological approach, there is also a sense in which the Macs of the world can be seen to perform a vital and necessary function in maintaining the life of the group. Vain as Mac's dream may be, to the extent that it serves to raise the morale of the group by giving it something in which to believe, something for which to fight, the dream may actually enhance its chances of survival. For although Mac trades on hope, it could be argued that things could not be otherwise if the group, if the species is to survive. Steinbeck goes so far as to speculate that "when our species developed the trick of memory and with it the counter-balancing projection called 'the future' this shock absorber, hope, had to be included in the series, else the species would have destroyed itself in despair." (SC, 86) As often as he reiterates the view that hope "manages to warp our whole world," (SC, 86) he opposes to it the countervailing notion that "our little mechanism, hope," was "achieved in ourselves probably to cushion the shock of thought." (SC, 86)

If Mac's brutality is an inevitable accompaniment of teleological thinking, it is also related to the fact that he is, in some fundamental way, "an expression of group-man." He is "a cell endowed with a special function, like an eye cell" (IDB, 151) and in performing that function he betters the chances of group survival. He is the perfect response to the conditions which have produced him.

Mac not only knows what to do, but also what to say in any given situation. He has a knack for saying exactly what the group would say if only the group could speak. He not only sees for the group, he thinks and speaks for the group as well—in the idiom it understands. His ability to fall in with the speech of the group is established early in the book when he first makes contact with the crop tramps. He knows how to strike just the note calculated to arouse their dormant sense of class consciousness or to instill in them a feeling of group solidarity.

"Can a guy join this club?" Mac asks the hoboes when he first makes contact with them, "Or does he got to be elected?"

When the answer comes, "Ground's free, mister," Mac chuckles. "Not where I come from."

A moment later when he offers his tobacco he says, "Would any of you capitalists like a smoke?"

As the sack of tobacco makes its rounds one of the man asks him, "Just get in?"

Mac answers, "Just. Figure to pick a few apples and retire on my income."

His efforts are rewarded when his questioner bursts out angrily, "Know what they're payin', fella? Fifteen cents, *fifteen lousy cents*!" (IDB, 56-57)

Doc has observed this quality in Mac. "You're a mystery to me," he tells Mac. "You imitate any speech you're taking part in. . . . You're an actor."

"No," said Mac. "I'm not an actor at all. Speech has a kind of feel about it. I get the feel, and it comes out perfectly naturally. I don't try to do it. I don't think I could help doing it." (IDB, 148)

Mac makes up his tactics as he goes along. At one point when Jim asks him "How we going to go about it, Mac? What do we do first?" Mac explains, "We just have to use any material we can pick up. That's why all the tactics in the world won't do it. No two are exactly alike." (IDB, 37)

When Mac first arrives in the hobo jungle he finds the men apathetic and listless. Each man is insular, wrapped up in his own affairs. When he sees an opportunity to gain the confidence of a man named London—a kind of natural leader to whom the rest of the men look up, Mac leaps at the chance. London's daughter-in-law is in labor and is about to give birth to her baby with nothing more than a dirty and untrained midwife in attendance. Although Mac has no previous medical experience, he ousts the midwife and takes over the delivery himself. By this simple act he rouses the men to think and act as a group. He takes command, putting them to work building fires, gathering the necessary items. He makes a direct appeal to their sense of group identity.

"We're a bunch of lousy crop tramps. O.K. They won't help us. We got to do it ourselves." The words "lousy crop tramps" though insulting when used by the owners or vigilantes have the opposite effect when uttered by one of their own. And Mac knows it.

"The men seemed to stiffen a little, to draw closer together. The apathy began to drop from them. They hunched closer to the fire . . . A change was in the air. The apathy was gone from the men. Sleepers were wakened and told, and added themselves to the group. A current of excitement filled the jungle, but a kind of joyful excitement. Fires were built up. Four big cans of water were put on to boil; and then cloth began to appear. Every man seemed to have something to add to the pile. One took off his undershirt and threw it into the water and then put his shirt on again. The men seemed suddenly happy. They laughed together as they broke dead cottonwood branches for the fire." (IDB, 62,63)

After the delivery Mac gives the order to burn all the extra cloth donated by the men. Jim is puzzled by the order which seems unnecessarily wasteful.

"You didn't need all that cloth. Why did you tell London to burn it?"

"Look, Jim. Don't you see? Every man who gave part of his clothes felt that the work was his own. They all feel responsible for that baby. It's theirs, because something from them went out to it. To give back the cloth would cut them out. There's no better way to make men part of a movement than to have them give something to it. I bet they all feel fine right now." (IDB, 67)

He goes on to make the point even more explicitly.

> "Men always like to work together. There's a hunger in men to work together. Do you know that ten men can lift nearly twelve times as big a load as one man can? It only takes a little spark to get them going. Most of the time they're suspicious, because every time someone gets 'em working in a group the profit of their work is taken away from them; but wait till they get working for themselves. Tonight the work concerned them, it was their job; and see how well they did it."(IDB, 67)

It is not altruism, but necessity which motivates Mac. Yet his behavior is, in a sense, disinterested. He sees the interests of the group as the higher good and where those interests are involved he is single-minded to a fault. He takes the risk of delivering the baby in order to win the confidence of the hoboes and especially of their leader. "Course it was nice to help the girl," he tells Jim, "but hell, even if it killed her—we've got to use anything."

His rationale is clearly stated a moment later: "With one night's work we've got the confidence of the men and the confidence of London. And more than that, we made the men work for themselves, in their own defense, as a group. That's what we're out here for anyway, to teach them to fight in a bunch." (IDB, 66)

If one is seeking a biological or naturalistic allegory, Mac's role as midwife in the delivery of London's grandchild is perhaps intended to be symbolic of his role as midwife not only to the strike which he helps to bring into being but also to the to the new society which is struggling to be born. As midwife to the revolution Mac has a role to play and he plays it superbly.

Mac's ability to make the most of every opportunity, to be ruthlessly pragmatic where the welfare of the group is concerned, suit him perfectly to his function. Although he shows a certain amount of deference when Jim Nolan introduces him to an old top-faller named Dan, who had worked with the Wobblies in the north woods, he is more concerned with present potential than with past performance. He tells Jim to concentrate on the younger, more militant workers: "Don't waste your time on old guys like that. He's no good. You'll get yourself converted to hopelessness if you talk to old men. They've had all the kick blasted out of 'em." (IDB,79) However, when Dan falls from a tree and breaks his hip, Mac instantly turns the situation to account, exploiting the natural anger of the men who blame the company for providing a defective ladder. Dan's accident proves to be the spark that sets off the strike.

Mac's tactics gradually begin to pay off. In the beginning, the crop tramps lack all semblance of organization. Gradually they begin to shake off their apathy and take the first painful steps toward social cooperation. Under the tutelage of the Communist organizers the strikers develop from a shabby and apathetic mob into a highly organized social unit with planning, direction, and discipline, capable of providing for itself and administering to the needs and wants of the group.

Mac is sensitive to the mood of his hoboes in the way a well trained general is sensitive to the mood of his soldiers. He moves among them, listening, observing, taking note of their condition. He charts the rise and fall of their militancy the way a doctor charts the rise and fall of a patient's temperature. When the breaks fall his way, Mac knows how to take advantage of them, and when there are no breaks he sets about to create them.

Mac sees the strike as merely one of many small-scale, local battles in a class war. His concern is ultimately with the larger dimensions of the struggle. Whether the strike is lost or won is secondary to him. Success is to be measured in terms of the extent to which the hoboes and workers have gained a sense of their group identity and have succeeded in learning how to work together and fight together.

"We're getting the stiffs used to working together," he tells London at one point, "getting bigger and bigger bunches working together all the time, see? It doesn't make any difference if we lose. Here's nearly a thousand men who've learned how to strike. When we get a whole slough of men working together, maybe—maybe Torgas Valley, most of it, won't be owned by three men. Maybe a guy can get an apple for himself without going to jail for it, see?" (IDB, 290)

When Jim asks him if they should fight or just fade, pointing out that when the sheriff's detachment comes "through with guns they're going to kill a lot of our guys," Mac answers, "Suppose they do kill some of our men? That helps our side. For every man they kill ten new ones come over to us. The news goes creeping around the country and men all over hear it and get mad. Guys that are just half-warm get hot, see?"(IDB, 328)

The notion that Mac has no real interest in the workers and that he is merely using them for his own ends is pretty general among Steinbeck critics. But such an interpretation loses sight of the fact that Mac is, as Doc describes him, an emanation of group-man. As strategist for the group, Mac must look beyond the immediate needs of this or that individual or faction. He must, in his own fashion, attempt to see the larger picture in order to achieve the higher good. It follows from this that if the ultimate value is the survival of an entire class, individuals or even groups must sometimes be sacrificed to it. In *Sea of Cortez*, Steinbeck speculates that "weaker or slower units may even take their place as placating food for the predators for the sake of the security of the school as an animal." (SC, 240-41)

As an emanation of group-man, Mac adopts this reasoning as his own. At one point, Doc expresses his sympathy for a grower named Anderson whose crop and barn had been destroyed in a fire set by the vigilantes. Anderson had allowed the strikers to use his land in return for having his crop harvested and thus earned the wrath of the fruit growers. Mac had done all in his power to forestall vigilante action against Anderson—even to setting out a guard—but he justifies the result in a way that approximates Steinbeck and Ricketts in Sea of Cortez:

> "We can't help it, Doc. He happens to be the one that's sacrificed for the men. Somebody has to break if the whole bunch is going to get out of the slaughter-house. We can't think about the hurts of one man. It's necessary, Doc." (IDB, 207)

Mac does not hesitate to apply the same reasoning to Joy or Jim Nolan or even to himself. Indeed, as Communists, they suffer special penalties and disabilities, they run special risks. Early in the strike they are identified and marked out for torture or extermination by both the police and vigilante units which work in close cooperation with one another. "We're takin' you God-damn reds to the Vigilance Committee," a deputy tells them, "if you're lucky they'll beat the crap out of you and dump you over the county line; if you ain't lucky, they'll string you up to a tree. We got no use for radicals in this valley." (IDB, 156) Although they manage to escape on this occasion they know that from that time on they are marked men.

Mac and Jim work on in the knowledge that even their own side hates them.

"Jim said, 'Harry told me right at first what to expect. Everybody hates us, Mac.'

'That's the hardest part,' Mac agreed. 'Everybody hates us; our own side and the enemy. And if we won, Jim, if we put it over, our own side would kill us. I wonder why we do it. Oh, go to sleep!'" (IDB,293)

Mac foresees and accepts his fate with equanimity. When London expresses concern for one of the strikers who is being sought for both arson and murder, Mac says, "Don't give it a thought. Somebody'll kill him sometime, like that little guy Joy. He was sure to get popped off. Me an' Jim'll go that way, sooner or later. It's almost sure, but it doesn't make any difference." (IDB, 293)

Both Joy and Jim Nolan are killed in the course of the strike but their obligation to the group does not end with death. Joy's corpse is hardly cold before Mac proposes that the strikers set about staging a public funeral in order to win sympathy for their cause. When one of the strike leaders attacks him, snarling contemptuously, "Want to make a show of it, do you?" Mac answers without hesitation:

> "You're damn right!... What we got to fight with? Rocks, sticks. Even Indians had bows an' arrows. But let us get one little gun to protect ourselves, an' they call out the troops to stop the revolution. We've got damn few things to fight with. We got to use what we can. This little guy was my friend. Y'can take it from me he'd want to get used any way we can use him. We *got* to use him." (IDB, 175)

In the all-out war between the classes Mac must make use of any means at hand to keep the level of militance high. Despite the uneasiness of some of the other men he insists on opening the coffin and inspecting Joy's remains. "I want to see if it'd be a good idea for the guys to look at him tomorrow," he tells the others. "We got to shoot some juice into 'em some way. They're dyin' on their feet." (IDB, 209) When Doc Burton gently chides him, accusing him of wanting to see his old comrade for the last time, Mac answers: "If Joy can do some work after he's dead, then he's got to do it. There's no such thing as personal feelings in this crowd. Can't be." (IDB, 209-10)

With each passing day the situation grows more desperate for the strikers. Their food supplies are exhausted. They are unable to crack the united front of the big land owners because the valley is too well organized against them. When Doc disappears, under circumstances which suggest his abduction, Mac sees that it is only a matter of time before the growers declare them a menace to the health of the community and drive them out of the county. But even before that can happen the man whose land they are occupying orders them to vacate his property, and the police announce their plan to drive them out with guns if they do not leave voluntarily.

The theme of blood sacrifice occurs with increasing frequency in the final pages of the novel. Blood, or the sight of blood, is the stimulus that transforms the strikers from a shambles of hopeless men into a deadly fighting machine. Periodically, the group animal, as Doc refers to it, seems to require the stimulus of violence to keep the level of its militance high. Hungry, rained-out, all but starving, the strikers can only be stirred to action by a shock to their basic animal natures. References to group-man or to the mob as an animal occur all through the concluding pages of *In Dubious Battle*. Even Mac, who earlier registered his sharp disagreement with Doc over this very question, now admits the charge.

When Jim tells him that the mob which attacked the police barricade "was just one big animal, going down the road. Just all one animal." Mac answers,

> "That's right, what you said. It is a big animal. It's different from the men in it. And it's stronger than all the men put together. It doesn't want the same things men want—it's like Doc said—and we don't know what it'll do." (IDB, 322-23)

His words echo a warning issued early in the novel by the old topfaller, Dan. In the general misery, he tells Jim, "It's like the whole bunch, millions and millions was one man, and he's been beat and starved, and he's gettin' that sick feelin' in his guts." (IDB, 73) And he adds prophetically. "When that big guy busts loose, there won't be no plan that can hold him. That big guy'll run like a mad dog, and bite anything that moves. He's been hungry too long, and he's been hurt too much; and worst of all, he's had his feelings hurt too much." (IDB, 73)

Mac himself says what amounts to the same thing in a conversation with Jim, for although Mac speaks for the group and acts for the group, he can neither predict its behavior nor control the direction it will take. He freely admits this, telling Jim, "If I could tell in advance what a bunch of guys'd do, I'd be president. Some things I do know, though. A smell of blood seems to steam 'em up. Let 'em kill somethin', even a cat, an' they'll want to go right on killin'." (IDB, 310)

Even as they sit talking the mob, which has over-run the police barricade is on its way back, bent on attacking them.

"It'll get that barricade," said Jim.

"That's not what I mean. The animal don't want that barricade. I don't know what it wants. Trouble is, guys that study people always think it's men, and it isn't men. It's a different kind of animal. It's as different from men as dogs are. Jim, it's swell when we can use it, but we don't know enough. When it gets started it might do anything," (IDB, 323)

Mac touches on this theme once more when he tells Jim and London about the hideout he is preparing against the day when the mob may turn on them in earnest if the strike breaks up.

"We'll see how our guys feel. If they're sore and mean, we'll fight. But if they look yellow, we'll clear out, if we can." He tells London. "If that happens. you and me and Jim have to go quick and far. That mob's going to want a chicken to kill, and they won't care much who it is." (IDB, 310)

Mac works to squeeze the last bit of resistance out of the workers even when the strike is clearly lost. It is his hope that they will stand their ground and provide an example of militance to the rest of the working class. He tells Jim,

> "If we sneak off and the word gets around, and men say 'They didn't even put up a fight,' why all the working stiffs will be unsure of themselves. If we fight, an' the news gets around, other men in the same position'll fight too." (IDB, 328)

But in the face of the overwhelming force arrayed against them he seems unable to rally the workers for their last great battle. Defeated and hungry, their luck run out, the strikers are unsure whether to fight or run. It is at this point that the fruit grower's association plays into Mac's hands by providing him with the incident he needs to touch off the spark of resistance. An ambush in the night, a shotgun blast in the dark, and the strike yields up another blood victim. Lured out by a vigilante ruse, Mac and Jim leave the protection of the camp when they are told that Doc Burton has been found injured in the fields. The ambush succeeds. Jim is cut down by a shotgun blast which catches him full in the face. The vigilantes escape in the dark.

Mac carries his dead partner back to the camp and slings him onto the platform. He places the lantern "so that the light fell on the head." In the dark circle beyond the light of the lantern the hoboes and crop tramps, the migrants and bindlestiffs gathered to take their final lesson in militance: Mac speaks for the group:

"Comrades! He didn't want nothing for himself——" (IDB, 349)

OF MICE AND MEN

One of the seeming paradoxes about John Steinbeck is that he sometimes employs the device of allegory to expound a philosophy of naturalism. In *Of Mice and Men* he employs the device of the many-leveled story to illustrate the workings of natural law and to construct an anti-utopian fable.

The plot of the novel is easily told, for there is a minimum of action, a minimum of characterization. The main interest in the work centers around the relations between George and Lennie and the special dream they share of saving up enough money to buy a piece of land where they can live out their days in peace and security. Although physically huge and powerful, Lennie has the mind of a child and needs someone to look after him. George has taken care of him ever since the death of his last relation left him alone and virtually helpless. Out of their deep and powerful hunger for a place where they can belong, they have woven an improbable fantasy of a mythical farm where they can settle down and leave off their wandering and rootless existence. *Of Mice and Men* tells the story of the tragic end to their dream, for the plan goes awry and the dream fails when Lennie's well-meaning efforts to be friendly end in the death of a ranchman's wife.

On one level *Of Mice and Men* is a tale of lonely tramps who bounce from one job to another, who follow the harvest from cotton to wheat with no end to their wanderings in sight. "Guys like us, that work on ranches, are the loneliest guys in the world. They got no family. They don't belong no place." (1)

With his superhuman strength and his subhuman intelligence Lennie is too patently a creature of allegory for the reader to be long confused on this point. As to the exact nature of the allegory or symbolism however, there was confusion and even dissension. This chorus of criticism apparently intimidated Steinbeck himself as he indicated in a letter to his agents: "I probably did not make my subjects and my symbols clear. . . . apparently I did not get it over."

What Steinbeck failed to get across, or what his readers failed to perceive, was the utopian or millennial aspect of the dream. For "the earth longings of a Lennie," as Steinbeck wrote in the same letter to his agents, were to represent "the inarticulate and powerful yearning of all men."

On the primary level the dream which Lennie and George create represents an expression of their desire to end their aimless wandering. "We'd jus' live there," George tells Lennie. "We'd belong there. There wouldn't be no more runnin' round the country." (OMM. 101-102) On the secondary, or allegorical level, the story of George and Lennie, the failure of their dream, is intended to suggest the precarious nature of all existence. Their plight, like that of the mouse in Burns' poem, is symbolic of the human condition at large.

The universality of the dream is made clear by Crooks, the Negro stableman, when he tells Lennie,

> "I seen hunderds of men come by on the road an' on the ranches, with their bindles on their back an' that same damn thing in their heads. Hunderds of them. They come, an' they quit an' go on; an' ever' damn one of 'em's got a little piece of land in his head." (OMM, 129)

He implies that the dream is utopian, that it is unattainable—"Never a God damn one of 'em ever gets it." (OMM, 129) He has seen men "Nearly crazy with loneliness for land, but ever'time a whore house or a blackjack game took what it takes." (OMM, 134) The utopian or millennial equation is made complete when he tells Lennie: "Just like heaven. Ever'body wants a little piece of lan'." (OMM, 129) And he adds, "It's just in their head. They're all the time talkin' about it, but it's jus' in their head," (OMM, 130)

On the allegorical level, George and Lennie's dream represents man's quest for the kingdom of heaven on earth—the earthly paradise where perfect love and justice will prevail. On this level George has much in common with what Steinbeck has elsewhere described as the "feeders of hope." It is he who feeds Lennie's hope, and he makes the dream believable when he tells it. Whenever Lennie asks for a retelling of the dream George asks him,

> "Why'n't you do it yourself? You know all of it." But Lennie answers, "No. . . . you tell it. It ain't the same if I tell it." (OMM, 30)

The vision of the farm serves to keep Lennie in line just as the promise of heaven operates as a moral check on the behavior of the mass of mankind. When George is pleased with Lennie he dangles the vision of the farm before his eyes:

> "Good boy! That's fine, Lennie! Maybe you're gettin' better. When we get the couple acres I can let you tend the rabbits all right. Specially if you remember as good as that." (OMM, 31)

But just as the sinner who transgresses against the moral code is threatened with the loss of eternal life, Lennie is threatened with dire consequences when he misbehaves. George warns him, "But you ain't gonna get in no trouble, because if you do, I won't let you tend the rabbits." (OMM, 32)

The essence of the telling is repetition and reiteration—a quality common to religious or Biblical utterance. The dream always takes the same form and begins in the same way. First there is George's disgust with Lennie which serves as the necessary prelude to forgiveness.

> "God a'mighty, if I was alone I could live so easy. I could go get a job an' work, an' no trouble. No mess at all, and when the end of the month come I could take my fifty bucks and go into town and get whatever I want." (OMM, 23-24)

When George has sufficiently vented his anger and Lennie is sufficiently contrite, his despairing question, "George, you want I should go away an' leave you alone?" (OMM, 26) elicits the answer he seeks. George tells him that they are family and will always stay together. George's mood softens and the way is prepared for the telling of the dream. The recitation which follows immediately after, has all the earmarks of a religious ritual. Once George has forgiven Lennie and begins to tell the dream, his voice changes and his manner becomes studied and formal.

> "George's voice became deeper. He repeated his words rhythmically as though he had said them many times before. 'Guys like us, that work on ranches, are the loneliest guys in the world. They got no family. They don't belong no place. They come to a ranch an' work up a stake and then they go into town and blow their stake, and the first thing you know they're pounding their tail on some other ranch. They ain't got nothing to look ahead to.'" (OMM, 28)

As the recitation proceeds, the angry words with which George first chided Lennie undergo a subtle transformation. His complaint which starts out-

> "I could stay in a cat house all night. .. .Get a gallon of whiskey, or sit in a pool room and play cards or shoot pool." (OMM, 24)

is gradually transformed into its opposite-

> "We don't have to sit in no bar blowin' our jack jus' because we got no place to go."(OMM, 29)

As George contrasts their state with that of the other ranch hands— "With us it ain't like that. We got a future." (OMM, 28)—Lennie becomes more and more excited. George tells him:

> "'If them other guys gets in jail they can rot for all anybody gives a damn. But not us.' Lennie broke in. 'But not us! An' why? Because. . .because I got you to look after me, and you got me to look after you, and that's why.' He laughed delightedly." (OMM,29)

Gradually, George works around to the dream of the future—perfect and free of contradiction. As they approach the climax of the dream, as the vision of paradise draws nearer, Lennie's ejaculations become more and more ecstatic:

> "'Someday—we're gonna get the jack together and we're gonna have a little house and a couple of acres an' a cow and some pigs and—'
> *An' live off the fatta the lan'* Lennie shouted. 'An' have *rabbits*. Go on, George! Tell about what we're gonna have in the garden and about rabbits in the cages and about the rain in the winter and the stove, and how thick the cream is on the milk like you can hardly cut it. Tell about that, George.'"(OMM, 29-39)

The content of the dream is fairly well fixed. Whenever George forgets or leaves out part of it Lennie is quick to prompt him.
It is a romantic retelling of the American past:

> "I could build a smoke house like the one gran'pa had." (OMM, 101)

It recalls a time of innocence and childhood.

> "An' we'd keep a few pigeons to go flyin' around the win'mill like they done when I was a kid." (OMM, 103)

It invokes in some sense the agrarian myth of the garden:

"An' when we kill a pig we can smoke the bacon and the hams, and make sausage an' all like that. An' when the salmon run up river we could catch a hundred of 'em an' salt 'em down or smoke 'em. We could have them for breakfast. They ain't nothing so nice as smoked salmon. When the fruit comes in we could can it—and tomatoes, they're easy to can. Ever' Sunday we'd kill a chicken or a rabbit. Maybe we'd have a cow or a goat, and the cream is so God damn thick you got to cut it with a knife and take it out with a spoon." (OMM, 101)

Marx once characterized religion as "the opiate of the masses." To Steinbeck and Ricketts teleological constructions, whether religious or utopian, are alike in that they are all, at bottom, outgrowths of "causal thinking warped by hope." (SC, 56) They are the perennial refuge of the downtrodden and the oppressed, the compensating dream of the defeated, of those who have nothing to lose but their hope.

Those for whom the dream holds the greatest appeal are the defective, the defeated, the maimed. When Candy, the one-armed swamper, overhears George describing the farm to Lennie, he asks, "You know where's a place like that?" (OMM, 104) Like George and Lennie, he yearns for a place where he will "belong" and where he will still be welcome when he gets too old to work.

"They'll can me purty soon," he tells them, "Jus' as soon as I can't swamp out no bunk houses they'll put me on the county." (OMM, 106) His fear is that when that happens "I won't have no place to go, an' I can't get no more jobs." (OMM, 107) He begs to be let into their plans. "Maybe if I give you guys my money, you'll let me hoe in the garden even after I ain't no good at it. An' I'll wash dishes an' little chicken stuff like that. But it'll be our own place, an' I'll be let to work on our own place." (OMM, 106)

Their dream is of a place where they can belong, where no one can shove them around. "It'd be our own, an' nobody could can us," George tells Lennie.

"If we don't like a guy we can say, 'Get the hell out,' and by God he's got to do it. An' if a fren' come along, why we'd have an extra bunk, an' we'd say, 'Why don't you spen' the night?' an by God he would." (OMM, 103)

For a fleeting moment, as Candy proffers his money, their quest seems almost at an end, the holy grail seems almost within their grasp. Their mood, as befitting such an occasion, is one of reverent wonder.

"They looked at one another, amazed. This thing they had never really believed in was coming true. George said reverently, 'Jesus Christ! I bet we could swing her.' His eyes were full of wonder." (OMM, 106)

The ambivalence with which men sometimes approach that vision is suggested by the tone of cynical disbelief with which Crooks at first dismisses the dream. When Lennie and Candy inadvertently reveal their secret Crooks interrupts their reverie to scoff at their plans.

"You guys is just kiddin' yourself. You'll talk about it a hell of a lot, but you won't get no land. You'll be a swamper here till they take you out in a box. Hell, I seen too many guys. Lennie here'll quit an' be on the road in two, three weeks." (OMM, 132)

But Crooks, too, is one of the maimed, one of the defeated. Although he has "read plenty of books" and knows well enough that "it's just in their head" (OMM, 130) he cannot live without hope any more than the rest of mankind. When Candy and Lennie convince him that they have almost enough money to buy the land, his cynicism gives way before the need and the yearning which he shares with the rest of the men. As he asks to be let into their dream he unconsciously touches his hand to his deformed and twisted back.

In *Of Mice and Men* Steinbeck tells two stories to make a single point illustrating the larger context of natural law in which the fate of mice as well as men is decided. The stories of Candy's dog and of Lennie are parallel illustrations of the same principle at work. The first presents it on the level of the lower animals, the second translates it into human terms. The fate of the dog helps us understand the fate of the man. Both dog and man come under the judgment of nature, and both are eliminated—the dog because he is blind and aged, Lennie because he is mentally deficient.

The relationship between Candy and his dog illuminates the relationship between George and Lennie and helps define the nature of George's responsibilities to his charge. Candy has had the dog with him ever since it was a pup, just as George has taken care of Lennie since he was a boy. Lennie follows George everywhere he goes and reposes in him the blind trust and loyalty that a dog reposes in his master. Both George and Candy accept responsibility for their charges, and in return both enjoy their love and devotion. Both are spared the loneliness and sense of hopelessness which assails the other ranch hands.

When it becomes necessary for George to kill Lennie in order to spare him further suffering, his responsibility in the matter is defined in terms of an earlier scene in which Candy's dog must be killed after it becomes obvious that it is too old to go on living. Both acts are in the nature of mercy killings, and both are called for by the family code. But Candy fails in his obligation to put his dog out of its misery "I ought to of shot that dog myself," Candy tells George at one point. "I shouldn't ought to of let no stranger shoot my dog." (OMM, 108)

Thus initiated, thus instructed, George fulfills his obligation to the letter. Once again, the parallelism is so precise as to admit of no other construction. Borrowing the very pistol which had been used to put down the dog, George uses it to put Lennie out of his misery as the vigalantes close in on him. He carries out the sentence of death according to the precise formula given earlier. Speaking of Candy's dog.

> "Carlson said, 'The way I'd shoot him, he wouldn't feel nothing. I'd put the gun right there.' He pointed with his toe. 'Right back of the head. He wouldn't even quiver.'" (OMM, 82)

The dog and the man suffer an identical fate and in both instances it is Slim, the jerk-line skinner, who acts as final judge and arbiter in providing warrant for the act.

Slim occupies a unique place in the structure of the allegory. On the primary level he is the jerk-line skinner, "capable of driving ten, sixteen, even twenty mules with a single line to the leaders. He was capable of killing a fly on the wheeler's butt with a bull whip without touching the mule." (OMM, 61-62) He was, Steinbeck tells us,

> "the prince of the ranch. . . . There was a gravity in his manner and a quiet so profound that all talk stopped when he spoke. His authority was so great that his word was taken on any subject, be it politics or love." (OMM, 61-62)

Slim stands high in the hierarchy of powers as well as the hierarchy of men. He represents an unknown and therefore mysterious quantity. At one point, when Curley seems about to pick a fight with him, one of the characters says,

> "Curley's just spoilin' or he wouldn't start for Slim. An' Curley's handy, God damn handy. Got in the finals for the Golden Gloves. . . . But jus' the same, he better leave Slim alone. Nobody don't know what Slim can do." (OMM, 96)

The qualities which account for his stature among the men elevate him to an eminence on the allegorical level as well. He represents the authority from which there is no appeal. To the men, "Slim's opinions were law." (OMM, 81) It is he who decides the fate of Candy's dog and, by extension, of Lennie as well.

We first see Slim carrying out the judgment of nature when his own dog gives birth to nine pups. He destroys four of them "right off," because, "she couldn't feed that many." (OMM, 65) The line of thought so explicitly developed in *Sea of Cortez* is made implicitly here. Conditions being what they are, there is not enough food for all the pups, and so Slim destroys four, saving those which are, in his judgment, best fitted for survival. "'Got five left, huh?' one of the men asks him. 'Yeah five. I kept the biggest.'" The needs of the mother also figure in his thinking. He plans to keep the pups for "a while so they can drink Lulu's milk."(OMM, 65)

When the fate of Candy's dog comes up for consideration, it is Slim who sits in judgment on the case and renders the final verdict. Carlson initiates the proceedings, complaining that he cannot stand the stink of the aging animal. He argues that the dog is too old to go on living and should be destroyed for its own good:

> "'Got no teeth,' he said. 'He's all stiff with rheumatism. He ain't no good to you, Candy. An' he ain't no good to himself. Whyn't you shoot him, Candy?'" (OMM, 80)

Candy tries desperately to save the dog, but Carlson presses the attack relentlessly. He offers to shoot the dog himself and assures Candy that the dog won't feel a thing. During the discussion of the dog's fate, Slim speaks only once, but his words have all the weight of a sentence of death.

> "Carl's right, Candy. That dog ain't no good to himself. I wisht somebody'd shoot me if I get old an' a cripple." (OMM, 81)

From that sentence the old man knows there is no appeal: "Candy looked a long time at Slim to try to find some reversal. And Slim gave him none. At last Candy said softly and hopelessly, 'Awright—take 'im.'" (OMM, 85)

The mysterious nature of Slim's powers, his calm, benign manner, his deific countenance, are alluded to again and again. Steinbeck describes him as having "calm, God-like eyes." (OMM, 72) So great is his power that even George comes under his spell. He forgets his fears and tells him all about how Lennie and he got into trouble on their previous job and had to leave town under the cover of night. And when George tells Slim how he used to play jokes on Lennie because he "was too dumb to take care of himself," his voice begins to take on "the tone of confession." (OMM,72)

If, on the allegorical level, Slim represents some higher power of nature—of "God" perhaps—in philosophical terms he represents the principle of non-teleological thought. He looks on life with "calm eyes" seeing things as they are. Instead of the "fierce but ineffectual attempt to change conditions which are assumed to be undesirable," he practices the "conscious acceptance" that Steinbeck sees as "a desideratum, and certainly as an all-important prerequisite," of non-teleological thought. (SC,135) In opposition to George, who offers another example of "causal thinking warped by hope," Slim represents the principle of harmonious accommodation to the universe.

Steinbeck is aware that individuals who employ non-teleological thinking

> "will be referred to as detached, hard-hearted, or even cruel. Quite the opposite seems to be true. Non-teleological methods more than any other seem capable of great tenderness, of an all-embracingness which is rare otherwise." (SC, 146)

Steinbeck goes to some lengths to clear Slim of any imputation of hard-heartedness. He is far from callous or indifferent to the suffering which takes place around him. As Carlson leads the old dog out to be shot, Slim endeavors to spare Candy whatever pain he can.

Slim said, "Carlson."
"Yeah?"
"You know what to do."
"What ya mean, Slim?"
"Take a shovel," said Slim shortly.
"Oh, sure! I get you." He led the dog out into the darkness. (OMM, 269)

As the men sit waiting for the sound of the shot that will tell them Carlson has finished off the dog, Slim cannot keep his hands from twitching.

"A minute passed, and another minute. Candy lay still, staring at the ceiling. Slim gazed at him for a moment and then looked down at his hands; he subdued one hand with the other, and held it down." (OMM,87)

Again, at the very conclusion of the book, after George has shot and killed Lennie, it is Slim who reassures him and reaffirms the correctness of his action, saying to him, "You hadda, George. I swear you hadda." (OMM, 186)

If Slim plays a role similar to that of Doc Burton in the novel *In Dubious Battle*, George fulfills a function not unlike that of Mac. As Mac leads the crop tramps—the big guy—by holding up before them the promise of a time when "maybe a guy can get an apple for himself without going to jail for it," George leads Lennie—the big guy—by holding out the promise of a future in which Lennie will get to tend the rabbits.

The dream may serve as a moral check or encourage men to work together, but it cannot save them from the defects of their nature or the consequences of their behavior any more than it can suspend the operation of natural law or hold in abeyance the forces that work for change. The shimmering dreams of the millennium can only end in death, yet only death, it seems, can end them. Rooted as they are in half-truths and fed on empty hopes, the "best laid schemes" of men as well as mice "gang aft a-gley."

The theme is a perennial one. "The lad that hopes for heaven," Housman once wrote, "Shall fill his mouth with mould." Man can no more hope to avoid "the thousand natural shocks the flesh is heir to" than the field mouse, most insignificant of creatures, can hope to avoid the plowman's point. "*Nobody never gets to heaven,* an' nobody gets no land," Crooks observes in *Of Mice and Men*.

There is no sadder or sterner, no more trenchant judgment on millennialism in all American literature than that implicit in the final scene of Steinbeck's work.

As George raises the Luger which he had stolen from Carlson, ready to fire it "at the place where the spine and the skull were joined,"

(OMM, 182) the final telling of the dream takes place amid ironic echoes of the Twenty-third Psalm:

> "The Lord is my shepherd;
> I shall not want.
> He maketh me to lie down in
>   green pastures;
> He leadeth me beside the still waters . . . "

George directs Lennie to turn his head and look across at the pool, across the still waters of the river, promising to tell him "so you can almost see it." (OMM, 181)

"'We'll have a cow,' said George. 'An' we'll maybe have a pig and chickens . . . an' down the flat we'll have a . . . little piece alfalfa—'
'For the rabbits,' Lennie shouted.
'For the rabbits,' George repeated." (OMM, 182)
They reconstruct the ritual, recreate the dream for the last time.
"When we gonna do it?"
"Gonna do it soon."
"Me an' you."
"You . . . an' me." (OMM, 183)

It is the vision of heaven in the split second before eternity. As Lennie looks across the river, like he "can almost see the place." George tells him once more of the perfect place where love abides forever.

"'Ever'body gonna be nice to you. Ain't gonna be no more trouble. Nobody gonna hurt nobody nor steal from 'em.'
Lennie said, 'I thought you was mad at me, George.'
'No,' said George. 'No, Lennie. I ain't mad. I never been mad, an' I ain't now. That's a thing I want ya to know.'"(OMM, 183)

As the voices of the posse tracking Lennie down come closer, George raises the gun and brings the muzzle close to Lennie's neck.

"The hand shook violently, but his face was set and his hand steadied. He pulled the trigger. The crash of the shot rolled up the hills and rolled down again. Lennie jarred, and then settled slowly forward to the sand, and he lay without quivering." (OMM, 184)

THE GRAPES OF WRATH: *THE THIRTIES*

Perhaps no novel since *Uncle Tom's Cabin* or Bellamy's *Looking Backward* has struck the public consciousness with the force of *The Grapes of Wrath*. Certainly no other novel to come out of the 'thirties, when books on social themes were legion, provoked such public outcry or aroused such earnest social speculation. Steinbeck's description of conditions in the dust bowl area evoked disaster on an epic scale and struck a responsive chord in the hearts of men and women who had seen their own hopes blasted by the operation of impersonal forces. His moving portrait of a people in flight across the land—the images he conjured up of young and old piled into steaming wrecks; of women, cadaverous, the hope gone dead in their eyes; of men stuck, mired in despair, uncomprehending of it all—all these, recalled and reinforced by newsreel and photo magazine, summed up the brooding sense of failure which afflicted an entire generation in those years when it seemed the depression would never end.

The novel was an immediate best-seller and its publication resulted in a massive outpouring of sympathy for the migrant. Almost over night the Okies became a national by-word, and Steinbeck's reputation as a social critic seemed established beyond cavil. Never was an audience readier to receive an author's message, or to read in its own if need be. Readers and critics alike, judging his work within the context of the 'thirties, took *The Grapes of Wrath* to be a vehicle of partisan social propaganda. The Associated Farmers of Kern County, the locale of some of the action in *The Grapes of Wrath*, condemned the book as one which would "incite hatred and eventually lead to the support of subversive activities." A headline writer for one Midwestern newspaper went so far as to proclaim that Steinbeck had urged a "Marxist Uprising," while Bernard DeVoto called the book "Judgment, propaganda, and manifesto all in one."

No doubt Steinbeck was gratified by the fact that he had succeeded in focusing national attention on the plight of the migrants, but the charge that *The Grapes of Wrath* was a partisan social tract must have been a bitter pill for him to swallow. Although few people knew it at the time, it was his unwillingness to publish a purely propaganda novel that had led him to abandon the completed manuscript of *L'Affaire Lettuceberg*, an earlier work on the same subject. He had destroyed the book because, as he wrote in a joint letter to his agent and publisher, "it isn't honest . . . I'm not telling as much of the truth . . . as I know."

It was not that he had falsified anything—"the incidents all happened," but the result of limiting the picture, the effect of his omissions, had been to encourage a sense of responsibility or blame-feeling which could only result in heightened hostility. The aim of *L'Affaire Lettuceberg*, as he acknowledged to his correspondents, was "to cause hatred through partial understanding"—ironically, almost the identical charge the Associated Farmers were later to lay against *The Grapes of Wrath*.

They could hardly have been more wrong.

In *L'Affaire Lettuceberg* Steinbeck had allowed his indignation at the treatment of the migrant workers to run away with him. He had fallen into the trap of teleological thinking—of causal thinking which led to the assigning of blame and the inciting of hatred. In *The Grapes of Wrath* he set out to correct the errors he had fallen into in *L'Affaire Lettuceberg* and return to his own work ethic, his own "work drive," which "aimed at making people understand each other."

Steinbeck once wrote of *In Dubious Battle* "I guess it is a brutal book, more brutal because there is no author's moral point of view." *The Grapes of Wrath* clearly has an author's moral point of view, and far from being brutal can only be described as compassionate. In *The Grapes of Wrath* Steinbeck sought to tread the middle ground between the moral indignation to which he had succumbed in *L'Affaire*

Lettuceberg and the moral detachment which some professed to see in his earlier work *In Dubious Battle*.

In writing *The Grapes of Wrath* it was Steinbeck's intent to comprehend a larger picture than he had in the abandoned work—one which would eschew partial answers and avoid placing blame. It was his intent to point to the existence or operation of factors not customarily considered and to show the Okies as unwitting participants in a movement, vast in scope, brought on by severe disturbances in both the economy and ecology of man. To this end he included within the framework of the book a series of intercalary chapters or sociological interludes, as they have been called, in which he could range beyond the limits customarily imposed upon the novel.

In the intercalary chapters he was able to present the larger context of ecological factors within which the westward migration took place. The ultimate villain or source of the problem was not to be identified as any one individual or class–instead one gradually became aware of a complicated interaction of natural and social forces—a kind of super-organism or super-mechanism—which played a decisive part in driving the Okies from their lands and reducing them to the status of migrants.

The sociological interludes also enabled Steinbeck to portray the mentality and practices of representative figures in the economic establishment from land office clerks, bankers, businessmen, up to the higher echelons of the California Fruit Growers' Association, spokesman and agent for the absentee landlords of California. And while he does not treat the owners in anything like the depth he accords the Okies, whose courage and endurance he commemorates in the stoic heroism of the Joads, he nevertheless attempts, in certain crucial sections, to indicate his belief that the owners, no less than the Okies, are caught up in a gigantic play of forces beyond their ability to comprehend or their power to oppose.

The migrants' struggle to survive fills him with a sense of wonder. Admiration for their courage and compassion for their suffering invest the book with a kind of epic grandeur. At the same time, *The Grapes of Wrath* like *In Dubious Battle*, attempts to suggest the essentially organic and inter-related nature of the social process and to point up the folly of short-range, teleologically based answers. In *In Dubious Battle* Steinbeck had carried the fight to the social utopians. *The Grapes of Wrath* carries it to the Social Darwinists. As Doc, in his debates with Mac, points out the unrealistic nature of utopian solutions, Steinbeck, in his monologues to the owners, points to the inevitable consequences of their short-sightedness which is storing up the grapes of wrath, creating "armies of bitterness." Their refusal to take account of what "is," he tells them, has the effect of hastening on the very thing they dread most.

> "If you who own things people must have could understand this, you might preserve yourself. If you could separate causes from results, if you could know that Paine, Marx, Jefferson, Lenin, were results, not causes, you might survive. But that you cannot know." (1)

Far from seeking to lay blame or arouse hostility by providing partisan or one-sided "answers," Steinbeck intended in *The Grapes of Wrath* to help people to understand one another. In the context of the times his warnings to the owners were interpreted as open advocacy of violent revolution, his depiction of what would happen to them if they persisted in their course was construed as a call to arms on the barricades of a new social utopia. However, when considered within the larger context of his thought in this period it may be seen that the action and argument of *The Grapes of Wrath* do not run counter to the non-teleological method of thinking which he explores in the earlier work, *In Dubious Battle*. Such biologically derived themes as ecological balance, survival of the fittest, dominance and regression, as well as the concept of group-man, which are the subject of searching speculation in *Sea of Cortez*, are basic elements in the plot of *The Grapes of Wrath* as well.

Ecology and Economy: The Grapes of Wrath opens with a brief but vivid description of the drought of the 1930s which devastated a vast extent of the Great Plains area, driving hundreds of thousands of persons off the land and rendering them a homeless, migratory population. It closes with a description of torrential rains and floods in California which reduce the already hungry and homeless Okies to the level of brute animal existence. Sandwiched between these two extremes of natural catastrophes are dozens of episodes, concrete and generalized, in which Steinbeck shows the Joads and other migrants at the mercy of social as well as natural forces. By showing the migrants at the mercy of natural phenomena Steinbeck underscores the dependence of all living things on the primal forces of nature. At the same time he points to the larger context in which institutions exert their influence. In Steinbeck's view the various levels of behavior form an integrated and interrelated whole. Social competition, the social process, parallels biological competition, but at the same time it meshes and blends with it. In this relationship, Steinbeck assigns primacy to the biological. He sees sociological phenomena as basically set within the context of the biological. Economic competition is a subset or extension of biological competition within the framework of which economic phenomena work out their expression of basic biological realities.

"Ecology has a synonym which is ALL," Steinbeck was to write in Sea of Cortez, and the ecological and historical events which he describes in The Grapes of Wrath were the result of a combination of factors which date back at least as far as the original cultivation of the Great Plains area, if not farther. The dust storms which reached such proportions in the 'thirties that at one point the Texas legislature conducted its sessions while wearing gas masks, were long in the making, and human behavior played its part in the process. For although low rainfall conditions are chronic in the Great Plains area, the dust bowl as such was the result of a complicated interaction of social and natural forces on a scale too vast to be contained in any "partial answer." In the larger picture, the Okies and their forbears had also had a hand in the events which led to their destruction, for by farming land which was marginal at best they had unwittingly contributed to the conditions which helped to bring on the dust bowl. Steinbeck hints at this when he has one of his characters say:

> "I know this land ain't much good. Never was much good
> 'cept for grazin'. Never should a broke her up. An' now
> she's cottoned damn near to death." (GW, 64)

In an article which appeared in *Scientific Monthly* in July, 1938, M.M. Leighton, while noting the cyclical pattern of low rainfall conditions in the Great Plains area, states that nonetheless,

> "the general prevalence of a definite soil profile over the
> Great Plains, and even the High Plains, shows that their
> climate is not too dry for a general vegetative cover to
> develop if it is allowed to do so. Man's activities, carried
> on without knowledge of or regard for the economy of
> nature, are responsible for dust storms of modern times."
> (2)

And he adds:

"Man's work is a new and powerful geological factor which must be used with caution." (3)

Other studies hint at the economic factor, noting that in periods of high prices and unusual demands for food supplies agriculture is extended into these marginal lands, thereby setting up the conditions which will result in dust storms during the next dry cycle. (4)

But the forms and levels cross over—one affects the other. It was not the dust storms alone which drove the Okies from the land. Steinbeck describes in some detail the impersonal action of the banks which, together with the dust bowl conditions, worked inexorably to accomplish the dispossession of the Okies.

> "A man can hold land if he can just eat and pay taxes;
> he can do that. Yes, he can do that until his crops fail
> one day and he has to borrow money from the bank."
> (GW, 43)

Once a man has mortgaged his land to the bank he is no longer wholly independent. He becomes a kind of extension of the bank's operation; he becomes, in effect, its tenant. If his crops continue to do poorly or if the market declines, he will be forced deeper and deeper into debt. If the process of borrowing goes on long enough he may be reduced to the status of a sharecropper with little more than a sentimental claim on the land which now belongs wholly to the bank or land company. Once this happens his fate is not longer in his own hands, he is no longer free to decide for himself whether to remain on the land or to leave it, for he is at the mercy of an impersonal economic process which operates with a cold mathematical rigor. Like the "owner men" who carry out the bidding of the machine even when they hate what it does, he has become the slave of a "cold and powerful" master which is as different from him as anything can be.

In Chapter Five, Steinbeck describes an owner's attempt to explain the workings of a bank to a tenant he has come to dispossess. A bank or a company, the owner tells the tenant is different from men:

> "Those creatures don't breathe air, don't eat sidemeat. They breathe profits; they eat the interest on money. If they don't get it, they die the way you die without air, without sidemeat. It is a sad thing, but it is so. It is just so." (GW,43)

Since the bank is not made of flesh and blood it has no feelings, it has only the profit motive to drive it faster and faster. If the bank does not turn over profits fast enough under the tenant system, if falling prices and a declining market threaten the margin of profit, the bank will be forced to seek more efficient means of farming the land. It will foreclose on the land and drive the tenant from his ancestral home.

"Well, the folks that owns the lan' says, 'We can't afford to keep no tenants.' An' they says, 'The share a tenant gets is jus' the margin a profit we can't afford to lose.' An' they says. 'If we put all our lan' in one piece we can jus' hardly make her pay.' So they tractored all the tenants off a the lan'." (GW,64)

Steinbeck sees the Joads as units in a vast collectivity caught up in the play of irresistible forces. A complex of natural and social forces working in tandem with the demand for seasonal labor in California combine to drive them from their homesteads and turn their footsteps westward in a movement unparalleled since the closing of the frontier. Like thousands of others they are pulled this way and that, their fate determined by forces beyond their understanding or control.

They are "movin' 'cause they got to. That's why folks always move." (GW, 173) But the reasons for their behavior, the forces which are operating on them are hidden from the Joads as they are from the lower orders. The complicated nature of the process and the scale on which it takes place, is too large to be understood by any but the most critical observer.

Casy, the itinerant preacher, tells Tom Joad:

> "An' if ya listen, you'll hear a movin', an' a sneakin', an' a rustlin' an'—an' a res'lessness. They's stuff goin' on that folks doin' it don't know nothin' about—yet." (GW, 237)

For the most part the Joads move without a plan, "jus' puttin' one foot in fronta the other." as Tom Joad tells Casy. (GW,236) But a common fate has driven them on the road and the lines of force are pulling them all in the same direction. Casy tells Tom:

> "Them people layin' one foot down in front of the other, like you says, they ain't thinking' where they're goin', like you says—but they're layin' 'em down in the same direction, jus' the same." (GW, 236-37)

Steinbeck centers his attention on the Joads but theirs is not an isolated example

> "66 is the path of a people in flight, refugees from dust and shrinking land, from the thunder of tractors and shrinking ownership, from the desert's slow northward invasion, from the twisting winds that howl up out of Texas, from the floods that bring no richness to the land and steal what little richness is there. From all of these people are in flight, and they come into 66 from the tributary sideroads. 66 is the mother road, the road of flight." (GW,160)

Lured westward by the orange handbills promising jobs and good living conditions in California, the migrants act out their drama on a national scale. Gradually, the sense of a whole country scurrying like lemmings before the onslaught of predators, begins to dawn on the Joads. As Jim Casy, who has been counting the cars of the migrants, begins to comprehend the proportions of the movement in which they are involved, he exclaims,

> "Tom, they's hunderds a families like us all a-goin' west. I watched. There aint none of 'em goin' east—hunderds of 'em. Did you notice that?"
> "Yeah, I noticed."
> "Why—it's like—it's like they was runnin' away from soldiers. It's like a whole country is movin'."
> "Yeah," Tom said. "They is a whole country movin'. We're movin' too." (GW, 235-36)

Again and again Steinbeck evokes the ecological or biological parallels. The cars of the migrant people "crawl" out of the side roads and creep "like bugs to the westward." As darkness overtakes them they cluster "like bugs near to shelter and to water." (GW, 264) As the migration gains momentum, a long thin trail of them stretches all the way from the Great Plains to the coast. "And in California the roads full of frantic people running like ants to pull, to push, to lift, to work." (GW,324)

Historical parallels alternate with biological models. At times Steinbeck likens the influx of dust bowl refugees to an invasion of ants, at times he sees them as the 'new barbarians' who will wrest the land from the soft-living native Californians if the process continues long enough.

Dominance and Regression: Again and again in the cycle of work which occupied him between 1934, when he commenced work on In Dubious Battle, and 1941, when Sea of Cortez appeared, Steinbeck alludes to the fierceness of the competition for survival. His acquaintance with Ricketts, his interest in Darwin and in natural studies had led him to see the numerous parallels between the conditions to be observed in the tide pools of the California coast and those to be found in the neighboring coastal valleys where men and animals, descended from earlier marine forms, fought and died on the land in a competition for existence no less ferocious than that of the sea. The theme of Darwinian competition with its ebb and flow of life forms also led him to postulate certain parallels with historical cycles of dominance and regression, and the fate of Rome and other great empires which had risen for a time to enjoy unchallenged supremacy only to fall before the onslaught of a younger and more vigorous people.

His biological studies led him to the conclusion that challenge, danger, and the stimulation resulting from the exposure to hardship were vital factors in the competition for survival, and this provided him with a basic biological rationale by which to explain the rise and fall of those cultures in which the accumulation of great wealth with the resulting diminution of challenge had led to a weakening of the moral and social fiber.

Describing the conditions he discovered at Puerto Refugio he writes:

> "In this harbor there were conditions of stress, current, waves, and cold which seemed to encourage animal life. And it is reasonable that this should be so, for active, churning water means not only a strong oxygen content, but the constant movement of food. And in addition,

> the very difficulties involved in such a position—necessity for secure footing, crowding, and competition—seem to encourage a ferocity and a tenacity in the animals which go past survival and into successful reproduction." (SC,227)

By the same token he notes that "with warm water and abundant food, the animals may retire into a sterile sluggish happiness." (SC,227) In humans too, Steinbeck suggests that a certain level of challenge is essential to survival, while luxury and ease lead inevitably to disintegration and decay. He cites Tacitus to make his point:

> "This has certainly seemed true in man. Force and cleverness and versatility have surely been the children of obstacles. Tacitus, in the *Histories*, places as one of the tactical methods advanced to be used against the German armies their exposure to a warm climate and a soft rich food supply. These, he said, will ruin troops quicker than anything else." (SC,227)

Intrinsic to Steinbeck's method—a method, he tells us, "somewhat like that of Darwin on the *Beagle*"—was the habit of seeing "dominant species and changing sizes, groups which thrive and those which recede under varying conditions." (SC,60) In history as in biology, Steinbeck suggests, the "processes of coordination and disintegration follow each other with great regularity," and he adds: "We think these historical waves may be plotted and the harmonic curves of human conduct observed."

Steinbeck did not restrict the application of the theme to ancient civilizations alone. In *Sea of Cortez* he offered the following succinct summary of the theme of shifting dominance in terms which clearly recall the conflict between the Okies and the landowners of *The Grapes of Wrath*. Once again he begins with an example from marine biology before drawing the human parallel. The relevant sections follow:

"It is difficult, when watching the little beasts, not to trace human parallels. . . . The routine of changing domination is a case in point. One can think of the attached and dominant human who has captured the place, the property, and the security. He dominates his area. To protect it, he has police who know him and who are dependent on him for a living. He is protected by good clothing, good houses, and good food. He is protected even against illness. One would say that he is safe, that he would have many children, and that his seed would in a short time litter the world. But in his fight for dominance he has pushed out others of his species who were not so fit to dominate, and perhaps these have become wanderers, improperly clothed, ill fed, having no security and no fixed base. These should really perish, but the reverse seems true. The dominant human, in his security, grows soft and fearful. He spends a great part of his time in protecting himself. Far from reproducing rapidly, he has fewer children, and the ones he does have are ill protected inside themselves because so thoroughly protected from without. The lean and hungry grow strong, and the strongest of them are selected out. Having nothing to lose and all to gain, these selected hungry and rapacious ones develop attack rather than defense techniques, and become strong in them, so that one day the dominant man is eliminated and the strong and hungry wanderer takes his place." (SC,94-95)

In *The Grapes of Wrath* Steinbeck traces this pattern of emergent and declining groups as it obtained in California from the time of the earliest settlers to the period of the drought and the great depression.

"Once California belonged to Mexico and its land to Mexicans; and a horde of tattered feverish Americans poured in. And such was their hunger for land that they took the land—stole Sutter's land, Guerrero's land, took the grants and broke them up and growled and quarreled over them, those frantic hungry men; and they guarded with guns the land they had stolen. They put up houses and barns, they turned the earth and planted crops. And these things were possession, and possession was ownership.

"The Mexicans were weak and fed. They could not resist, because they wanted nothing in the world as frantically as the Americans wanted land." (GW, 315)

But the descendants of the men who had fought for the land and staked their claim in blood, the offspring of the hungry and rapacious horde which had driven out the Mexicans became the favored group for,

". . . with time, the squatters were no longer squatters, but owners; and their children grew up and had children on the land. And the hunger was gone from them, the feral hunger, the gnawing, tearing hunger for land, for water and earth and the good sky over it, for the green thrusting grass, for the swelling roots. They had these things so completely that they did not know about them anymore." (GW, 315)

And the settled native population of California underwent a slow transformation that kept pace with the social changes that took place around them. For, "no matter how clever, how loving a man might be with earth and growing things" the time came when "he could not survive if he were not also a good shopkeeper." (GW, 316) As the simple economy of agrarian trade and barter was transformed into the system of commodity production geared to the price system, the descendants of the original settlers became "little shopkeepers of crops, little manufacturers who must sell before they can make." (GW, 316)

By that time, Steinbeck writes, they had forgotten—or had never known—

" . . . the stomach-tearing lust for a rich acre and a shining blade to plow it, for seed and a windmill beating its wings in the air. . . . These things were lost, and crops were reckoned in dollars, and land was valued by principal plus interest, and crops were bought and sold before they were planted. Then crop failure and drought, and flood were no longer little deaths within life, but simple losses of money. And all their love was thinned with money, and all their fierceness dribbled away in interest." (GW,315-316)

The pattern of consolidation so familiar in history, the pattern in which the rich grew richer and the poor grew poorer and in which the lands were increasingly concentrated in the hands of fewer and fewer owners was repeated once more in California, for "as time went on, the business men had the farms, and the farms grew larger, but there were fewer of them." (GW,316)

In time "farming became an industry, and the owners followed Rome, although they did not know it. They imported slaves, although they did not call them slaves: Chinese, Japanese, Mexicans, Filipinos." (GW,316)

In time the inevitable disintegration that accompanies the decrease in challenge, the weakness that results from over protection, manifested itself in the descendants of the early settlers, and Steinbeck contrasts the "civilized" wants and desires of the native population with the primitive life demands of the "new barbarians" as he terms them.

"And while the Californians wanted many things, accumulation, social success, amusement, luxury, and a curious banking security, the new barbarians wanted only two things—land and food; and to them the two were one. And whereas the wants of the Californians were nebulous and undefined, the wants of the Okies were beside the roads, lying there to be seen and coveted." (GW, 318)

The ancestors of the Okies had taken their land from the Indians as the ancestors of the Californians had taken theirs from the Mexican population. In *The Grapes of Wrath* Steinbeck suggests that a new confrontation was shaping up between the descendants of the original California settlers, who had grown soft through overprotection, and the Okies, who were tried and tested in adversity.

THE GRAPES OF WRATH:
EXODUS AND MIGRATION

The appearance of *The Grapes of Wrath* opened a floodgate of Biblical interpretations. Critics rushed to point out the obvious parallels between the flight of the dust bowl refugees and the exodus of the Jews. Readers lost no time in pointing out the similarities between Jim Casy, the itinerant preacher and Jesus Christ (note the initials J.C.). A veritable wealth of material lay to hand, a rich vein of Biblical allusions was opened up and an entire industry of Biblical criticism sprang up in the wake of its publication.

There can be no doubt that Steinbeck made deliberate use of the Biblical tradition, as the very title of the book makes clear. By so doing he achieved several ends. First, by appealing to a body of literature at once familiar to the predominantly Christian audience about him he won an immediate and sympathetic hearing for the despised and hated Okies, for he reminded his audience that they were dealing not with representatives of an alien culture but with members of their own fellowship and persuasion. Moreover, by interpreting the experience of the Okies within the framework of the Jewish exodus, by evoking the numerous parallels between the suffering and tribulations of the Okies and those of the Jews in Biblical times Steinbeck no doubt hoped to re-establish the human dignity and stature of a group which had come to be looked upon as pariahs, as the new untouchables.

But to leave it at this is to ignore the larger context into which Steinbeck would fit both events—the exodus of the Jews and the flight of the dust bowl refugees.

There is a tendency in Judaeo-Christian culture to regard the experience of the Hebrews as an event arranged by the special intervention of the deity for the instruction of the rest of mankind and thus to interpret all other experience in terms of it. But such anthropomorphic projections have no place in a non-teleological approach and are manifestly antithetical to its spirit. The symbolic or allegorical content of *The Grapes of Wrath* is ultimately not Christian but Naturalistic. Interpretations which stress Christian or teleological themes and symbols while ignoring the non-teleological context in which they occur offer only a partial and therefore misleading view of the novels. From a biological and non-teleological perspective the slow and stubborn progress of the turtle Tom Joad picks up, and which eventually escapes, is no less marvelous an event than the migration of the Okies or the exodus of the Jews. Viewed in this light, the turtle is an embodiment, a symbol, an expression of the primal force which drives all life forms—the will to survive.

Steinbeck sees the exodus of the Jews and the flight of the dust bowl refugees as coordinate phenomena, parallel phases in the larger, repetitive patterns of the race in which peoples widely removed in time and temper may undergo a similar challenge, a similar threat to their survival. And just as the Jews were toughened and made more resourceful by the difficult conditions of life to which they were exposed in their flight across the desert, the Okies are toughened and conditioned by the hardships they undergo on the long trek to California. One by one the weaker die off or desert or are killed by the police until only the strongest remain.

As the migration tests and develops the ability of the individual to adapt to new physical conditions it also tests the ability of the group, the collective, to adjust to new social conditions. The new mode of existence calls forth new adaptations and new social attitudes, for the rules by which men governed their lives under the old arrangements no longer apply.

Steinbeck describes in considerable detail the process by which the Okies, like the Jews, develop a new group code, a new ethic to replace the one no longer serviceable to their needs. They start out as single families, as an uncoordinated swarm, but as they settle into their new way of life they evolve into a new social group with new mores, new norms. At the end of each day's run there was a new camp site to be found, a new world to be built, for wherever one car stopped others were not long in coming. In each such locale a new community sprang up out of the need of men to relate to one another and to establish codes by which to live.

> "Every night relationships that make a world established; and every morning the world torn down like a circus.
> At first the families were timid in the building and tumbling worlds, but gradually the technique of building worlds became their technique. Then leaders emerged, then laws were made, then codes came into being...." (GW, 265)

Within the framework of the Okies' westward migration Jim Casy's story illustrates the way in which new prophets arise to give new hope and new laws when the old laws are found inadequate. On the first night out the Joads are faced with the necessity of burying Granpa beside the road without benefit of medical certification. For a number of reasons it is imperative that they move on at once, yet they are uneasy at this departure from the norm. At last Tom Joad the elder says:

> "'I'm sayin' now I got the right to bury my own pa. Anybody got somepin' to say?'
> The preacher rose high on his elbow. 'Law changes,' he said, 'but 'got to's go on. You got the right to do what you got to do.'" (GW, 191)

The researchers of Biblical parallels have tended to see Jim Casy as the symbol if not embodiment of Jesus Christ and consequently to subsume his agony and martyrdom under the mantle of Judaeo-Christian mythology. As in the case of the Jews and the Okies there can be no doubt that the comparison was deliberate, but what is far more important from the standpoint of non-teleological philosophy is that Steinbeck intended to suggest the still higher level of abstraction under which both figures can be subsumed. This level embraces or includes not only Jesus Christ and Jim Casy but also Mac and Jim Nolan, the Communist organizers of *In Dubious Battle*. What is common to them all is that they belong to the tribe of prophets— "the feeders of hope" whether economic or religious, who keep the race alive by keeping hope alive.

Jim Casy's personal development, the religious crisis he undergoes, illustrates the stages through which a prophet passes as he moves from an old or outmoded religion which no longer has any relevance to the needs of the people, through a phase of doubt and questioning before arriving at a new faith or belief more immediate to the needs of the group.

In the foreword which he wrote for Rickett's book, *Between Pacific Tides*, Steinbeck spelled out the various stages of thought through which men pass in the course of their progress from believing to seeing. The passage is worth quoting here.

> "Periodically in the history of human observation the world of external reality has been rediscovered, reclassified, and redescribed.... The process of rediscovery might be as follows: a young, inquisitive, and original man might one morning find a fissure in the traditional technique of thinking. Through this fissure he might look out and find a new external world about him. In his excitement a few disciples would cluster about him and look again at the world they knew and find it fresh. From this nucleus there would develop a frantic new seeing and a cult of seers who, finding some traditional knowledge incorrect, would throw out the whole structure and start afresh. Then, the human mind being what it is, evaluation, taxonomy, arrangement, pattern making would succeed the first excited seeing. Gradually

the structure would become complete, and men would go to this structure rather than to the external world until eventually something like but not identical with the earlier picture would have been built. From such architectures or patterns of knowledge, disciplines, ethics, even manners exude. The building would be complete again and no one would look beyond it—until one day a young, inquisitive, and original man might find a fissure in the pattern and look through it and find a new world. This seems to have happened again and again in the slow history of human thought and knowledge."(1)

This passage appears to describe exactly the phases through which Jim Casey passes as he makes his way from old time religion through a patch characterized by moral neutralism and heightened sensual awareness before embracing a new social idealism.

When we first meet Casy he has lost his faith in the old dichotomies of good and evil. He no longer believes in either the deity or the dogma of Christianity, and no longer considers himself a preacher. He describes in detail to Tom Joad the route by which he has moved from faith to doubt. At first he was contrite and blamed himself for falling from grace but the more he reflected upon the matter the more aware he became of what seemed to be a fatal contradiction in the theory of his faith.

In an agony of religious doubt he had gone off into the hills, "thinkin', almost you might say like Jesus went into the wilderness to think His way out of a mess of troubles." (GW, 109) In the wilderness Casy had time to "give her a damn good thinkin' about," (GW,110) and re-established his sense of oneness with nature. There he faced up to the contradictions between what he preached and what he had observed at first hand about his own behavior and that of others.

"I says to myself, 'What's gnawin' you? Is it the screwin'?' An' I says, 'No, it's the sin.'" (GW,31)

Eventually he arrives at the point in his meditations where he rejects the dichotomy of sin and virtue and attempts to think in a non-teleological way - that is without either praising or blaming.

"Before I knew it, I was saying' out loud. 'The hell with it! There ain't no sin and there ain't no virtue. There's just stuff people do. It's all part of the same thing. And some of the things folks do is nice and some ain't nice, but that's as far as any man got a right to say.'" (GW,31-32)

Casy's progress is marked by the stages of his feeling about both prayer and preaching. There was a time before doubts intervened when prayer seemed the answer to everything. "I use ta think that'd cut 'er," he tells Tom Joad at one point:

> "Use ta rip off a prayer an' all the troubles'd stick to that prayer like flies on flypaper, an' the prayer'd go a-sailin' off, a takin' them troubles along. But it don' work no more." (GW,341)

His sojourn in the wilderness left him unable or unwilling to pray, since he no longer believes in either the tenets or the teaching of the church. His reluctance is evident each time he is called upon to officiate in some religious capacity. On the morning before the Joad's departure for California he is asked to say grace at breakfast. "I ain't a preacher no more," he tells them. But he consents to say a few words all the same.

> "If me jus' bein' glad to be here, an' bein' thankful for people that is kind and generous, if that's enough—why, I'll say that kinda grace. But I ain't a preacher no more."
> (GW, 109)

The grace that follows is unlike anything that the Joads have ever heard, for on the preacher's face, "there was a look not of prayer, but of thought; and in his tone not supplication, but conjecture." (GW, 109) Afterwards, Ma Joad says to Tom,

> "Curiousest grace I ever heard, that he gave this mornin'. Wasn't hardly no grace at all. Jus' talkin', but the sound of it was like grace." (GW, 126)

Like the grace which he offers at the Joad's breakfast table, the address Casy makes at Granpa's burial is hardly a prayer in the ordinary sense of the word—"it wasn't no preacher's prayer," Casy later tells Sairy Wilson. (GW, 297) Shorn of false sentiment and the customary religious flourish, it scrupulously avoids the elegiac tone.

"This here ol' man jus' lived a life an' jus' died out of it. I don' know whether he was good or bad, but that don't matter much. He was alive, an' that's what matters. An' now he's dead, an' that don't matter." (GW, 196)

Casy's refusal to pray for the dead suggests the finality of his break with the doctrines of orthodox Christianity. It signals his rejection of the traditional religious obsession with the question of death and the afterlife of the soul and points to his increasing involvement with the living in their struggle for survival. Granpa's work is simple, he tells them. "He got a job to do, but it's all laid out for 'im an' there's on'y one way to do it." (GW, 197) And he abruptly concludes his remarks, "An' now cover ' im up and let 'im get to his work." (GW, 197)

But although Casy no longer knows how to pray and no longer considers himself a preacher, the fact is, as Granpa observes early in the novel, "Once a fella's a preacher, he's always a preacher. That's somepin' you can't get shut of." (GW, 138) The force of habit is strong, and although Casy has "dropped the leading strings of a Sunday-school deity" he is "still led by the unconscious teleology" of his "developed trick." (SC,86) He carries over with him habits and mannerisms of the past. "Fella gets used to a way of thinkin', it's hard to leave," Casy admits. "I ain't a preacher no more, but all the time I find I'm prayin', not even thinkin' what I'm doin'." (GW, 65) Although he rejects the dead religious formulas of the past and can no longer pray in the traditional way, Casy still feels the need to lead the people, to minister to their needs.

In their first meeting he tells Tom Joad the spirit is still strong in him even though he "ain't so sure of a lot of things." (GW, 28) The spirit Casy refers to is the spirit of love—love of his people, not of dead institutions: "I says, 'What's this call, this sperit?' An I says, 'It's love. I love people so much I'm fit to bust, sometimes.'" (GW, 32)

Casy's passionate and loving nature is no more able to resist that call than the Joads can resist the forces impelling them to migrate, or the turtle can ignore the pull of primal forces which call it to its biological tasks. "Nobody can't keep a turtle," Casy tells Tom. "They work at it and work at it, and at last one day they get out and away they go—off somewhere." (GW,28)

Like the turtle, Casy worked at it and worked at it until he was able to break out of the web of fundamentalist dogma in which his loving nature has been kept prisoner. Once free, he retraces the ground covered in almost two hundred years of American religious debate culminating in the Transcendentalist doctrine that all men are a part of the over soul. Rejecting the dogma of traditional religion and the abstract love of a mythical deity, Casy rediscovers and re-institutes the doctrine of love of one's fellow man.

"An' I says, 'Don't you love Jesus?' Well, I thought an' thought, an' finally I says, 'No, I don't know nobody name' Jesus. I know a bunch of stories, but I only love people.'" (GW, 32)

Eventually he postulates a new synthesis in which the traditional notion of the deity plays no part and in which the Holy Spirit becomes the human spirit.

> "I figgered about the Holy Sperit and the Jesus road. I figgered, 'Why do we got to hang it on God or Jesus? Maybe,' I figgered 'Maybe its all men an' all women we love; maybe that's the Holy Sperit—the human sperit—the whole shebang. Maybe all men got one big soul ever'body's a part of.'"(GW,32-33)

In time he comes to think of himself and of all things, animate and inanimate as parts of a still larger unity—the totality.

"Sometimes I'd pray like I always done. On'y I couldn' figure what I was prayin' to or for. There was the hills an' there was me, an' we wasn't separate no more. We was one thing. An' that one thing was holy." (GW, 110)

Casy's views are so alien to the Christian orthodoxy, that Tom Joad warns him, "You can't hold no church with ideas like that."(GW,33)

In *Sea of Cortez* Steinbeck tells us that this sense of unity with all living things, the attempt to see the universe as a cohesive and interrelated whole in which all parts co-exist is congruent with the non-blaming aspect of non-teleological thinking. It has characterized the thoughts or attitudes of men of widely differing outlooks and temperaments he tells us:

> "The profound feeling of it made a Jesus, a St. Augustine, a St. Francis, a Roger Bacon, a Charles Darwin, and an Einstein." (SC,217)

So long as a man can hold to that vision, that higher synthesis, Steinbeck implies, he stands at the *summa* of human understanding—eschewing value judgments based on limited or partial understanding. So long as he can maintain such a stance a man would succeed in viewing all life with a calm and compassionate eye and avoid the inevitable inference of causality, responsibility and blame so characteristic of teleological thinking.

This non-blaming attitude of forgiveness which causes Jesus Christ to cry out "Forgive them father for they know not what they do" is echoed by Jim Casy at the moment he is struck down by a vigilante: "You fellas don't know what you're doin'." (GW, 527)

But every synthesis yields to a new thesis, and the necessity for acting, for choice-making, leads to the inevitable introduction of value judgments which polarize and harden into systems of belief based on the moral dichotomy of good and evil. Thus a Jesus or a Marx may attempt for a time to avoid making value judgments but inevitably both they and their followers, caught up in the process of life are forced down the same path at the end of which there beckons a heavenly after-life, free of all suffering, or an earthly paradise based on justice and reason.

Although Casy has worked his way out of the wilderness of fundamentalist dogma and embraced the doctrine of love he has not yet found a way to translate his belief in the fellowship of souls into a religion of service to the people. The spirit is still strong in him, but having discovered the irrelevancy of the old-time religion to the contemporary needs of the people—"Hope of heaven when their lives ain't lived? Holy Sperit when their own sperit is downcast an' sad?"(GW,71)-he does not know what to put in its place. He is no longer certain that he has anything to offer them, that he has any function to perform.

"Here I got the sperit sometimes, an' nothin' to preach about. I got to lead people, an' no place to lead 'em." (GW29)

It is the sight of the empty houses, the thought of the people who once lived in them that rekindles in him the hope that he may once again be of service to his people, that he may discover new meaning and purpose in his life and find a way to translate his new-found doctrine into action.

Casy's progress takes him from hope of a heavenly after-life, from an emphasis on death and resurrection to a concern with the living in their day to day struggle for survival. He has come to understand that he must move away from abstract speculation about God and Jews, that he must stop seeing things through the medium of a dead theory and must return to the vital and enduring source of all religions—the life of the people.

He recognizes that before he can preach again he must, in a sense, be born anew. He must abandon the graveyard of abstract dogma and return to the source of all religions, to the life of the people:

> "Gonna learn why the folks walks in the grass, gonna hear 'em talk, gonna hear 'em sing. Gonna listen to kids eatin' mush. Gonna hear husban' an' wife a-poundin'

the mattress in the night. Gonna eat with 'em an' learn."
His eyes were wet and shining. (GW, 128)

He understands that he must learn before he can preach, that he must study before he can teach. "I ain't gonna preach. . . . I ain't gonna baptize. . . . I ain't gonna try to teach 'em nothin'. I'm gonna try to learn," he tells Ma Joad. (GW, 127-28)
Henceforth, he determines, he will shut himself off from no experience common to man. He will put away his false sense of shame. "Gonna lay in the grass, open an' honest with anybody that'll have me. Gonna cuss an' swear an' hear the poetry of folks talkin'." (GW, 128)

A religion is never fresher, more potent, more viable than at the moment of its inception, at the moment of its break with the forms and traditions of the past. In his gratitude for his awakening sense of the joy in life and the rediscovery of love he hymns a paean of religious affirmation: "All that's holy, all that's what I didn't understand. All them things is the good things." (GW, 128)

Jim Casy's transit across the country parallels his transit across the terrain of religious philosophy. His movement is away from the dying and eroded fields where "the houses is all empty, an' the lan' is empty, an' this whole country is empty," to "where the folks is goin'."(GW,127) In a sense he leaves behind him the barren vineyards of orthodox theology for the newer and greener pastures of a fresh religion aborning: "I'm gonna work in the fiel's, in the green fiel's, an' I'm gonna be near to folks." (GW, 127-28)

The seed of Casy's new found religion of humanity awaits only transplanting to a new and fertile soil in order that it shall flower forth and yield the fruit of a new religion. It is in this context that the symbolic significance of the seed which is trapped in the shell of the turtle becomes clear. The chapter in which the turtle first appears opens with a description of

> ". . . sleeping life waiting to be spread and dispersed, every seed armed with an appliance of dispersal, twisting darts and parachutes for the wind, little spears and balls

of tiny thorns, and all waiting for animals and for wind, for a man's trouser cuff or the hem of a woman's skirt, all passive, but armed with appliances of activity, still, but each possessed of the anlage of movement. (GW, 20)

In the course of the turtle's progress "one head of wild oats was clamped into the shell by a front leg." (GW,21) After two encounters with automobiles the turtle successfully crosses the highway where

> "The wild oat head fell out and three of the spearhead seeds stuck in the ground. And as the turtle crawled on down the embankment, its shell dragged dirt over the seeds." (GW,22)

In this symbolic parallelism of cyclical regeneration the perambulating turtle represents the people in their westward migration. The seed is the seed of Jim Casy's philosophy which will take root and spring to new life in an ever-repeated cycle of the race. Tom Joad picks him up as he does the turtle, and the Joads deposit him in California as the turtle deposits the seed on the other side of the embankment. The seed of Casy's new philosophy, like the seed carried by the turtle, is enclosed in the dry and desiccated shell of a dead and withered growth—but it will, like the seed, spring to new and fruitful growth when it is planted in fresh soil.

When Casy goes to jail by intervening for another man who is wanted by the police, the transplantation is completed, for he is buried, in a sense, in the underworld of the jail house. In the jail house he learns things that he had spent years trying to figure out for himself. He tells Tom,

> "Here's me, been a-goin' into the wilderness like Jesus to try to find out somepin'. Almost got her sometimes, too. But it's in the jail-house I really got her." (GW,521)

Buried for a time in the rich and fertile soil of social discontent, the seed of Casy's new social vision takes root and begins to flourish, for he discovers that most of the men who are in jail are there "cause they stole stuff; an' mostly it was stuff they needed and couldn' get no other way." (GW,521) And he concludes: "It's the need that makes all the trouble." (GW,521)

In organizing a strike among the peach pickers, Casy attempts the first practical application of the principles of his new-found religion. By that act he completes the process of his own transformation from a Bible-belt evangelist to a strike organizer, from a disciple of orthodox Christianity to a disciple of humanity and a believer in some form of collective action.

Steinbeck's thesis that there is a fundamental similarity between the feeders of hope, economic and religious, is illustrated once again by the ease with which Casy makes the transition between the two. "Preachin's a kinda tone of voice, an' preachin's a way a lookin' at things," Tom Joad tells Casy at one point (GW,128), and the parallels between Mac and Jim Casy bear out this observation.

Mac, the atheistic Communist, falls readily into the style of pulpit oratory, while Jim Casy, the Bible-belt evangelist, falls as easily into the role of organizer and strike leader.

And just as Mac adopts the language and delivery of the revival meeting when he attempts to reach the strikers, Jim Casy embraces the theme of need and exploitation when he attempts to reestablish contact with the people. The ease with which the two men make the transition once again points up Steinbeck's thesis concerning the basic similarity of all teleologies. This essential similarity, this basic identity, is made manifest in a number of ways.

The parallels between Jim Casy and Jim Nolan, Mac's apprentice in *In Dubious Battle*, are also instructive. Like Jim Nolan, who renounces belief in orthodox religion only to embrace a new secular faith in communism, Jim Casy substitutes one religion for another. Moreover, Casy's denial of religious belief in the face of Sairy Wilson's request that he pray for her, echoes Jim Nolan's denial of religious belief in the face of Doc Burton's questioning. Jim Casy's denial, it may be added, is no more convincing than Jim Nolan's. The intersection of conflicting planes of reference, apparent in Jim Nolan's conversation with Doc Burton is also evident in the dialogue between Jim Casy and Sairy Wilson, who lies dying in her tent.

"I ast you to come to say a prayer."
"I ain't no preacher," he said softly. "My prayers ain't no good."
"I was there when the ol' man died. You said one then."
"It wasn't no prayer."
"It was a prayer," she said.
"It wasn't no preacher's prayer."
"It was a good prayer. I want you should say one for me."
"I don't know what to say . . . I got no God," he said.
"You got a God. Don't make no difference if you don't know what he looks like." (GW, 297-98)

Casy also learns as Jim Nolan did that the fate of a leader is to be rejected by the very group he seeks to help.

"Them very folks he been tryin' to help tossed him out. Wouldn' have nothin' to do with 'im. Scared they'd get saw in his comp'ny. Says, 'Git out. You're a danger on us!'" (GW, 524-25)

Like Mac and Jim Nolan he comes to accept the fact that the revolution devours its own children. Like them he has come to accept his fate as the price that must be paid for progress.

The culminating demonstration of the religious and teleological equation occurs at the very moment of his death, for Jim Casy—J.C., "the shiny bastard"—is damned by the agents of the peach growers as a "red son-of-a-bitch," (GW,527) just as Mac, the organizer of *In Dubious Battle*, is damned by the apple growers. And just as the apple growers kill first Joy, Jim Nolan and perhaps Doc Burton, the peach growers kill Jim Casy and mount a massive manhunt for Tom Joad who emerges to take the place of the fallen Casy.

Throughout the greater part of the novel Tom has functioned as a kind of devil's advocate of the practical man. Whenever Casy waxes ecstatic it is Tom Joad who brings him back to earth again. His pragmatic philosophy of "Layin' 'em down one at a time," his refusal to speculate about the future are opposed to Casy's constant speculation about what lies ahead and his restless habit of inquiring into everything happening around them.

When Casy gives voice to the doubt that lurks at the back of all their minds, "Well—s'pose all these here folks an' ever'body—s'pose they can't get no jobs out there?" Tom responds angrily, "Goddamn it!. . .How'd I know? I'm jus' puttin' one foot in fronta the other."(GW,236) When Casy says, ". . . when a fence comes up at ya, ya gonna climb that fence." Tom puts him off with, "I climb fences when I got fences to climb." (GW,237)

When he kills the man who has bludgeoned Casy to death he is forced to go into hiding. It is only then that he realizes how much he has come to respect Casy and even think like him. He is forced to go into hiding where he has time to reflect on the things that Casy taught him. In his last dialogue with his mother, Tom tells her how Casy told him that he tried to "find his own soul" and discovered that he had just "a little piece of a great big soul . . . Funny how I remember. Didn't even think I was listenin'. But I know now a fella ain't no good alone." (GW,570)

When Ma asks him what he is going to do, he tells her: "What Casy done."(GW,571) He reminds her of

> ". . . how it was in the gov'ment camp, how our folks took care a theirselves . . . I been wonderin' why we can't do that all over. Throw out the cops that ain't our people. All work together for our own thing—all farm our own lan'." (GW,571)

Tom's expresses his sense of identity with the group in terms of Casy's notion of the oversoul, but one can also hear in it echoes of the group commitment of Mac and Jim Nolan who expect to die in the struggle. When Ma expresses fear of what will happen to him, Tom answers her in words that echo those of the working class hero celebrated in the song of Joe Hill who was killed by the copper bosses.

"I dreamt I saw Joe Hill last night

> Alive as you and me
> Says I, but Joe you're ten years dead
> I never died says he . . .
> The copper bosses killed you Joe,
> They killed you, Joe, says I
> What they forgot to kill says Joe
> Went on to organize . . .
> From San Diego up to Maine
> In every mine and mill
> Where working men defend their rights
> It's there you'll find Joe Hill . . . "

Echoing that theme, Tom tells her it doesn't matter because he'll be everywhere:

> "Wherever they's a fight so hungry people can eat, I'll be there. Wherever they's a cop beatin' up a guy, I'll be there. If Casy knowed, why, I'll be in the way guys yell when they're mad an'—I'll be in the way kids laugh when they're hungry an' they know supper's ready. An' when our folks eat the stuff they raise an' live in the houses they build—why, I'll be there. See?" (GW,572)

The Determinates of Survival: If Jim Casy and Tom Joad feed the hopes and aspirations of the people, it is Ma Joad who attends to their immediate physical needs. Ma Joad epitomizes all that is best and most enduring in human values. She combines the tenderness and compassion of Doc Burton with the toughness and single-mindedness of Mac where the welfare of the group is concerned. When the interests of the family demand the sacrifice of one of its members, Ma Joad is equal to that too.

As they cross the desert on the last lap of their journey to California, Granma lies dying in one corner of the truck. Ma Joad remains at her side all through the long ordeal of her dying, concealing her death from the rest of the family as well as from the agricultural inspectors who stop them at the border. She knows that any delay is likely to prove fatal to their hopes. It is only after they cross the summit of the last range of mountains and the fertile valleys of California lay spread out below them that she tells them Granma is dead.

Ma Joad recognizes the power of the group when it is united, when all its members are pulling together. Early in the novel she tells Tom: "If we was all mad the same way...they wouldn't hunt nobody down." (GW,104) Near the end of the novel she expresses her faith that they will survive despite all their hardships: "Why, Tom—us people will go on livin' when all them people is gone. Why, Tom, we're the people that live. They ain't gonna wipe us out. Why, we're the people—we go on." (GW,383)

She does not scruple to ride rough-shod over the will of the others when the security of the family is threatened. When it is suggested that Tom and Casy should remain behind to repair the car while the rest of them proceed to California, she takes up a jack-handle to get her way. But despite all her efforts the family slowly disintegrates under the terrible burden of existence.

At the beginning of the novel Ma Joad is concerned only with the needs of her immediate family. When a group of hungry children gather around to watch the Joads at their meal, she decides to feed the family inside their tent, away from the watchful eyes of the children. But as the Joads help or are helped by others their sense of community is broadened far beyond the limits of the immediate family.

Ma Joad makes this clear near the conclusion of the novel when she tells the woman who has assisted in the delivery of her daughter Rose of Sharon's still-born baby: "Use'ta be the fambly was fust. It ain't so now. It's anybody. Worse off we get, the more we got to do."(GW,606)

Eventually the concept of the family is extended to embrace all those who are in need regardless of blood lineage. It is this larger sense of obligation, this larger idea of the family, which prompts Ma Joad's action in the final scene when, they come upon a dying man who has been starving himself in order to feed his child.

That ending, in which Rose of Sharon consents to nurse the starving man at her breast could not have failed to shock the western sense of morality. A more primitive people might have understood it without difficulty, might have accepted it without question. Indeed, anthropological literature offers numerous examples of primitive behavior in which just such a gift of the milk of a nursing mother forms the central part of a ritual of tribal adoption. But in a culture in which the female breast has come to be regarded primarily as an object of sexual, if not of commercial, manipulation, such a denouement, with its insistence on the more embarrassing aspects of man's animal nature seemed an affront to civilized sensibilities.

Numerous critics have joined in polemic over the significance of the scene in which Rose of Sharon consents to nurse a starving man at her breast. Those who have managed to come to terms with the ending seem often to have done so by interpreting it in terms of Biblical symbolism. Biblical overtones there are in plenty, but taken in the context of Steinbeck's often stated biological orientation it seems clear that Rose of Sharon, in that moment when she gives her breast is demonstrating something far more basic than Biblical symbolism.

From the shallow, self-centered young woman of the earlier chapters, from a superficial and self-indulgent girl who exaggerates every threat to her unborn child, Rose of Sharon has been transformed into the natural animal. Driven from her home by drought and flood, abandoned by her husband, denied even such primitive shelter as the Joads have managed to come by during the period of her labor, she, like the rest of them, learns to fight back for survival with all the courage and cunning of her animal nature. By giving the milk that would have gone to her still-born baby she demonstrates the capacity of the group to transcend the limits of conventional morality and draw upon its basic biological reserves when its survival is at stake.

That capacity, in Steinbeck's view, represents a basic index of the group's survival quotient. Steinbeck does not tell us whether the Joads will survive or not, but he does provide us with what he considers to be the determinates of that question. They will endure if they are fit to endure. They will survive if they are "armed for survival, fanged for survival, timid for it, fierce for it, clever for it, poisonous for it, intelligent for it." (SC,241)

For Steinbeck that final scene amounted almost to a profession of faith and it was as far as his faith would allow him to go.

CONCLUSION

Steinbeck once wrote of Ed Ricketts that "his scientific interest was essentially ecological and holistic. His mind always tried to enlarge the smallest picture." (1) He was, says Steinbeck, "an individualist who studied colonial animals with satisfaction,"(2) and although he held that "there is no creative unit in the human save the individual working alone," he understood that although it cannot create, the group, "can correlate, investigate, and build." (3)

Ricketts was "pleased with commensal animals, particularly with groups of several species contributing to the survival of all." He once wrote:

> "You know, at first view you would think that the rattlesnake and the kangaroo rat were the greatest of enemies since the snake hunts and feeds on the rat. But in a larger sense they must be the best of friends. The rat feeds the snake and the snake selects out the slow and weak and generally thins the rat people so that both species can survive. It is quite possible that neither species could exist without the other." (4)

This somewhat brutal example taken straight out of biology is crucial to an understanding of the ecological mindset which sees the universe as a harmony of contradictions, as a balance or equilibrium struck between apparently opposing, even contradictory tendencies. This same balancing of seemingly opposed tendencies or interests is manifest in Steinbeck's novels of this period as well. Just as *Sea of Cortez* balances the conflicting claims of competing species by stressing the commensal nature of certain relationships *In Dubious Battle* and *The Grapes of*

Wrath balance the conflicting claims and interests of competing groups within the same species-the crop pickers and the fruit growers, migrants and ranchers.

In the two novels Steinbeck occupies a position midway between the polar extremes of two opposing ideologies or teleologies-between the utopian visions of social reformers on the one hand, and the shortsighted self-aggrandizement of rugged individualists on the other. In Steinbeck's view neither side sees the whole picture. Just as Mac and Jim Nolan are prevented from seeing what "is" by the very nature of their commitment, the owners are cut off from a full understanding of the situation by the nature of their vested interest, for, as Steinbeck tells them, "the quality of owning freezes you forever into 'I,' and cuts you off forever from the 'we'." (GW, 206) In *The Grapes of Wrath*, Steinbeck, speaking through the medium of the intercalary chapters, directs the heavy artillery of his argument against the owners. Their refusal to take account of what "is," he tells them, has the effect of bringing about the very thing they dread most. But in *In Dubious Battle* the situation is just the reverse, for the crop tramps have in Mac and Jim Nolan two energetic and articulate spokesmen against whose oversimplified conceptions Doc, as Steinbeck's representative, does battle.

This tendency to balance or harmonize seemingly contradictory or opposing forces, this ecological and holistic approach, informs all the novels of the depression cycle. It is manifest not only in the way Steinbeck regards the interaction of competing groups and species, but in his conception of the relationship between the individual and the group as well. For as the individual struggles to find identity within the group, the group works ceaselessly to subordinate the interests of the individuals within it to the welfare of the group as a whole.

In *Sea of Cortez* Steinbeck balances his admiration for the gallantry, intelligence or ingenuity of the individual specimens he examines against the awe and wonder, the "satisfaction" with which Ricketts and he "studied colonial animals." In his fiction he balances his admiration for the courage or integrity of the individual against the awe and wonder with which he contemplates the social organization and stoical endurance of the group under stress.

This balance is apparent not only in the juxtaposing of *In Dubious Battle* against *The Grapes of Wrath*, it is manifest within the individual novels as well. In the former, Doc exemplifies the role of the critical individual intelligence while Mac epitomizes the organizing role of the social or group consciousness, but in the larger picture both exist together, both are necessary to the survival of the species. Something of this is suggested in the scene in which Doc points out to Mac that men are both individuals and cells in the group animal just as the cells of their own bodies are both individual cells and part of an organic whole.

It is this ecological and holistic approach, this balancing of seemingly opposing forces, which has made possible so many conflicting interpretations of Steinbeck's meaning. At the same time it has given rise to charges of confusion or inconsistency in Steinbeck's thought, for it is frequently argued that non-teleological or "is" thinking, which is an outgrowth of such an ecological approach, is incompatible with the social concern Steinbeck has manifested. Thus, Steinbeck's refusal to lay blame, taken in context with what Frederick Bracher refers to as "his fervent desire to correct social injustices" (6) has led many critics to infer a fundamental contradiction in the philosophical basis of his thought. As Bracher succinctly puts it:

> "An obvious corollary of the avoidance of cause-thinking and blame-feeling would be an inability to take sides. . . a quietistic acceptance of a larger pattern of which the two opposed sides are necessary parts. (7)

But if Ricketts and Steinbeck reject blame-feeling and cause-thinking—that is, the concept of "injustice" as a basis of action, it does not at all follow that they are thereby bereft of any other basis on which to take action-"to take sides." Bracher is not alone in imputing confusion to Steinbeck and Ricketts on this score, but as Bracher readily acknowledged, "Mr. Ricketts insists that this corollary is not justified and that non-teleological thinking is, in fact, the only solid basis for positive action." (8)

As Steinbeck and Ricketts saw it, the only solid basis for action lay in a full awareness of the ecological interaction or relationship of the groups under study. The key to their approach is provided in a passage quoted earlier describing the efforts of the Norwegian authorities to preserve the willow grouse from extinction by placing a bounty on the hawk. In that example the attempt to save the grouse by killing large numbers of the hawk, it will be remembered, had exactly the reverse effect, and Steinbeck and Ricketts made the point that cause-thinking and blame-feeling based on partial understanding lay at the root of the failure to solve the problem.

The rejection of blame-feeling did not lead to a "quietistic acceptance" as the corollary might imply. Instead, they proposed a non-causal, non-blaming approach capable of revealing the actual, rather than the presumed, nature of the relations between the two species of birds. In their view only such a non-blaming approach could provide a "solid basis for positive action" to save the grouse.

This non-blaming approach characterizes Steinbeck's approach to human relationships as well. He saw the need for reform in the system of California agriculture if certain basic conflicts and instabilities were not to destroy the fabric of society, but in his eyes only an ecological and holistic view could succeed in suggesting the nature of the relationship that obtained between the migrants and the landowners.

The California fruit growers as well as many readers interpreted his warnings as a call to arms to establish a collective society. (Steinbeck Urges Marxist Uprising, read one headline.)

"Do you know what they're afraid of," Steinbeck wrote in a letter to his agent Elizabeth Otis, "They think that if these people are allowed to live in camps with proper sanitary facilities they will organize, and that is the bugbear of the large landowner and the corporation farmer. The states and counties will give them nothing because they are outsiders. But the crops of any part of this state could not be harvested without them." (9)

The charge that he advocated some form of collectivism was absurd. Rather than urging collectivism, it is far more likely that he might have called for the breaking up of the large estates into smaller, family-owned units as one useful step. In *Sea of Cortez* he more than once expresses his doubts concerning the efficacy, durability, and desirability of the collective state with what he called its rigidity and tendency toward "overprotection" of the populace. He likens this social mutation to the thickening armor of the great lizards whose evolution in this direction assured their eventual extinction. Any tendency to overprotect the populace would, he felt, inevitably lead to weakness, decay, and disintegration. In this he clearly differed from some Marxists.

The thesis that he espoused a form of Social Darwinism also reveals certain obvious difficulties both practical and philosophical. In "Harvest Gypsies," Steinbeck not only attacked the shortsighted policies of the owners, which he saw as leading to the destruction of the civil peace, he also proposed a far-reaching program of reforms on behalf of the migrants, including government sponsorship of a network of migrant labor camps organized along the lines of the one he was later to describe in *The Grapes of Wrath*.

Herbert Spencer's many pronouncements on the evils of government intervention in any area other than the administration of justice are a matter of record. As Richard Hofstadter summed them up in *Social Darwinism in American Thought*:

> "Spencer deplored not only poor laws, but also state supported education, sanitary supervision other than the suppression of nuisances, regulation of housing conditions, and even state protection of the ignorant from medical quacks. He likewise opposed tariffs, state banking, and government postal systems." (10)

Certain aspects of the philosophy worked out by Steinbeck and Ricketts do indeed bear comparison with the ideas of Herbert Spencer. Both systems seek to achieve a grand synthesis, an all-embracing *Weltanschauung* in which the far removed and seemingly unrelated phenomena of the cosmos are brought into one vast and harmonious whole. Moreover, both systems lay great emphasis on the notion of a vital competition for existence which takes place on all levels of life. It was Spencer, after all, who coined the phrase "survival of the fittest," which Darwin admitted as more apt than his own term-"natural selection." (11) To go further, both systems view social phenomena and social organization in biological terms and both lay considerable emphasis on the significance of group behavior.

But despite certain correspondences between the two systems, the views espoused by Steinbeck and Ricketts differ in several basic essentials from the philosophy of Spencer. Spencer's notion that "the ultimate development of the ideal man is logically certain," (12) and his faith that progress was "not an accident, but a necessity...all of a piece with the development of the embryo or the unfolding of a flower,"(13) have no counterpart in the work of Steinbeck and Ricketts.

To Spencer it was clear that "evolution can only end in the establishment of the greatest perfection and the most complete happiness."(14) But such optimism finds no parallel in the thinking of Steinbeck and Ricketts. Their view of history envisions not progress but flux, not movement toward some happy plateau of biological perfection, but long term historical cycles in which social organization fluctuates between alternating phases of coordination and disintegration. Spencer's unquestioning assumption of the biological superiority of the dominant groups of his time, and his complete faith that they held the key to the future as well, assumed what remained to be proved in the course of further struggle. His argument, in effect, amounted to urging those in competition with the favored classes to cease striving for mastery on the grounds that the dominant classes were fittest to survive. The teleology of the argument is self-evident.

Steinbeck's thesis concerning the way in which the sons of the wealthy and successful are sometimes supplanted by the sons of the displaced groups runs exactly counter to Spencer's conviction that the dominant and ruling groups represent the highest achievement of the race and his assumption that they were, biologically speaking, fittest to survive. To Steinbeck and Ricketts, the notions of the rich and powerful, whether expressed in the religious accents of predestinarian Calvinism or of Social Darwinism must appear no less teleological than those of the poor and humble. For, as the hungry man dreams of food and the slave dreams of freedom, the well-fed and powerful dream of maintaining the *status quo*. If out of their dreams of bread or freedom the hungry man and the slave build their iron teleologies and fashion their myths of a heavenly or earthly paradise designed by God or history, the patrician, no less teleologically, concludes that his favored position is the clearest evidence of design and purpose in the universe.

If Steinbeck is to be compared to a Victorian thinker, perhaps it should be to Thomas Henry Huxley, Darwin's great defender. Huxley, an ardent advocate of social reform through state regulation was nevertheless aware of certain disturbing factors which reformers sometimes ignored. In 1888 he wrote,

> "Let us be under no illusions, then. So long as unlimited multiplication goes on, no social organization which has ever been devised, or is likely to be devised, no fiddle-faddling with the distribution of wealth, will deliver society from the tendency to be destroyed by the reproduction within itself, in its intensest form, of that struggle for existence the limitation of which is the object of society. And however shocking to the moral sense this eternal competition of man against man and of nation against nation may be; however revolting may be the accumulation of misery at the negative pole of society, in contrast with that of monstrous wealth at the positive pole; this state of things must abide, and grow continually worse, so long as Istar holds her way unchecked. It is the true riddle of the Sphinx; and every nation which does not solve it will sooner or later be devoured by the monster itself has generated." (15)

Teleological thinking places man at the center of the universe, makes man the measure of all things and tends to judge the universe in terms of its accommodation to his interests. Such thinking, while sometimes appearing in the guise of liberalism or modernism, usually ends up in a species of humanism so unyielding as to be almost theological in its rigidity. In the middle of the twentieth century the highest authority of Rome could affirm that in the divine and universal scheme of things plants were made for use of the animals and animals were made for the use and enjoyment of man.

But in non-teleological terms mankind is only *part* of the totality and the universe is neither constructed in its image nor managed in its exclusive interest. In the depression cycle Steinbeck sought consistently and conscientiously to present "the whole picture" which must include the needs, interests and interplay of all the competing species on earth. To Steinbeck and Ricketts only a non-teleological, ecological approach could hope to prepare one for such understanding.

Such an approach ultimately implies recognition-that is understanding or acceptance-of the fact that what may seem wasteful or injurious to one group or species may, in fact, seem useful or beneficial to some other.

In *Sea of Cortez*, Steinbeck and Ricketts record an experience which illustrates the various stages of thought through which they pass as they attempt to approach or approximate a sense of the whole. Encountering a fleet of Japanese fishermen busily dredging up the sea bottom, their first reaction is one of shock and outrage at their "wasteful" methods which threaten not only to wipe out the shrimp but to disturb the ecological balance of the area as well. The Japanese, they feel, are "committing a true crime against nature and against the immediate welfare of Mexico and the eventual welfare of the whole human species."(SC, 250)

In the second stage of thought they attempt to go beyond the question of blame, to consider what may be done to preserve a valuable source of food. Recognizing that the fisherman, as well as others involved in the operation, may be ignorant of the consequences of their behavior or may be acting in response to the immediate pressure of forces without taking into consideration long-range consequences, they propose that the Mexican Ministry of Marine, which had authority over these waters, should undertake a "careful study of this area. . ."so that "its potential could be understood and the catch maintained in balance with the supply. Then there might be shrimps available indefinitely." They note that "if this is not done a very short time will see the end of the shrimp industry in Mexico." (SC, 249-250)

The third stage or level is characterized by reflections of a more philosophical nature in which, leaving out their own notions of what ought to be, they attempt to gauge the effects of the shrimp fishermen's behavior on the totality. Here they are forced to the recognition or acceptance of the fact that although from a human point of view there is waste, to the totality everything is part of the process, and "to the whole, there is no waste."

"We tried to say that in the macrocosm nothing is wasted, the equation always balances. The elements which the fish elaborated into an individuated physical organism, a microcosm, go back again into the undifferentiated macrocosm which is the great reservoir. There is not, nor can there be, any actual waste, but simply varying forms of energy. To each group, of course, there must be waste-the dead fish to man, the broken pieces to gulls, the bones to some and the scales to others-but to the whole, there is no waste. The great organism, Life, takes it all and uses it all." (SC,263)

In this gradual unfolding of ascending or evolving states of consciousness, non-teleological thinking may be seen to bear a resemblance to certain Asian schools of thought wherein one mounts step by step or stage by stage from the primary level of self-consciousness to an awareness of or identification with ever larger and larger aggregations of the whole until, by the gradual annihilation or denial of the concrete and particular, as represented in the self, one approaches at last a consciousness of the totality and of one's identity with the unity or the whole.

To put it into Steinbeck's or Ricketts' scientific, biological, non-teleological terms,

> "A man looking at reality brings his own limitations to the world. Yet, if he has strength and energy of mind the tide pool stretches both ways, digs back to electrons and leaps space into the universe and fights out of the moment into non-conceptual time. Then ecology has a synonym which is ALL."(SC, 85)

On the popular level Steinbeck's depression novels are still widely regarded as examples of protest literature, but although the view of Steinbeck as a social critic is self-consistent on one level, and although his concern over the plight of the migrants was real enough and led him to oppose the short-sighted policies of the growers, he does not content himself with passing judgment on social institutions.

The works of the depression cycle are alike in their common concern for the lot of the dispossessed and disenfranchised migratory workers and in their compassionate consideration of the condition of all men, but what emerges at last as the central motif is a theme of perennial struggle, of mankind eternally engaged in dubious battle on the plains of heaven, or at least on the approaches to that earthly paradise of which men have so long dreamed. Steinbeck suggests that it is an indestructible dream, if an elusive one, for no sooner is the millennial faith of one age shattered on historical or political reality than the dream receives fresh interpretation at the hands of a succeeding generation.

It is the vision of heaven which Doc sees in the eyes of Jim Nolan and which, in one form or another, possesses George and Lennie as well as Jim Casy and the Joads. That vision is self-replenishing and springs spontaneously out of the conditions of man's life and the nature of his being. But the philosophical position which emerges with unmistakable clarity from Steinbeck's ecological novels stands in the most direct opposition to belief in Millenniums, whether secular or religious.

Flux is the order of the universe, change is the law of nature; that is the message Steinbeck relays. The vision of utopia is a fable, the promise of heaven is a fraud. Life has just "one commandment for living things: Survive!" (SC, 241)

ENDNOTES

CHAPTER ONE : (1) Malcolm Cowley, "Epilogue: New Year's Eve. "*Exile's Return* (2nd ed.; New York: The Viking Press, 1951), p. 293. (2) IV (Autumn, 1955) 210. (3) "A Postscript From Steinbeck," *Steinbeck and His Critics*, ed. E.W. Tedlock, Jr. and C.V. Wicker (Albuquerque: University of New Mexico Press, 1957), p. 307. (4) "About Ed Ricketts," *The Log From The Sea of Cortez* [New York: The Viking Press, 1951], p. xiv.

CHAPTER TWO: (1) John Steinbeck, *In Dubious Battle* (New York: Covici-Friede, 1936), p.211. Subsequent references to *In Dubious Battle* will be indicated by the symbols IDB and included in the text in parentheses. (2) John Steinbeck and Edward F. Ricketts, *Sea of Cortez* (New York: The Viking Press, 1941), p. 135. Subsequent references to *Sea of Cortez* will be indicated by the symbol SC and included in the text in parentheses

CHAPTER FOUR: (1) John Steinbeck, *Of Mice and Men* (New York: Viking Press, 1937), p. 28. Subsequent references to *Of Mice and Men* will be indicated by the symbol OMM, and placed in the text in parentheses

CHAPTER FIVE: (1) John Steinbeck, *The Grapes of Wrath* (New York: Viking Press, 1939), p. 206. (2) "Geology of Soil Drifting on the Great Plains." *A Companion to The Grapes of Wrath* (New York: The Viking Press, 1963), pp. 8-15.)

(3) *Ibid.*, p.15. (4) See Ivan Ray Tannehill. *Drought: Its Causes and Effects* (Princeton, New Jersey: Princeton University Press, 1948.) Portions of this monograph are reprinted in the Warren French *Companion* cited above, pp.5-8.)

CHAPTER SIX: (1) Foreword to Edward F. Ricketts and Jack

Calvin, *Between Pacific Tides*, 3rd ed. rev.; Stanford, California: Stanford University Press, 1952), p.v.
CHAPTER SEVEN: (1) "About Ed Ricketts," *The Log From The Sea Of Cortez* [New York: The Viking Press, 1951], p. liv. (2) *Ibid.*, p. xi. (3) *Ibid.* ,p.xlvi. (4) *Ibid.*, p.liv. (5) *Ibid*, p.xiv. (6) "Steinbeck and the Biologicial View of Man," Frederick Bracher in *Steinbeck and His Critics*, edited by Tedlock and Wicker, [University of New Mexico Press, 1957] p. 188 (7) *Ibid.*, p.187 (8) *Ibid.*, p.187 (9) Letter to Elizabeth Otis, quoted in *The Portable Steinbeck*, p. xxi (1O) 1st rev. cloth edition; New York: George Braziller, Inc.,1949) (11) Darwin to Lyell, Sept.28,1860: Life and Letters,II,p.346. Cited by Gertrude Himmelfarb, *Darwin and the Darwinian Revolution* [Garden City, New York: Anchor Books, Doubleday & Co.,1962]p.485) (12) *Social Statics* [New York: D. Appleton & Co.,1874], p.79) (13) *Ibid.*,p.80. (14) *First Principles* (4th Amer.ed.,1900, New York: D. Appleton & Co.),p.407.) (15) "The Struggle for Existence in Human Society, "*Selections From the Essays of T.H. Huxley*, edited by Alburey Castell [New York: Appleton-Century-Crofts, 1948], p.69.

Made in the USA
Lexington, KY
02 February 2013